T0319150

Connecting Your Students with the Virtual World

Make the most of today's technology to give your students a more interactive, authentic, global learning experience! *Connecting Your Students with the Virtual World* shows you how to plan themed projects for every season, embark on virtual field trips, and get students in touch with other classrooms worldwide. This updated edition includes a key new chapter on taking video conferencing to the next level for optimal student engagement and collaboration, as well as new chapters on connecting through games and esports and connecting with parents. The book includes a wide variety of standards-based, step-by-step activities you can implement immediately.

Billy Krakower is an educator and a national speaker and consultant. He is also the author of *Getting Started with STEM: Practical Strategies for the K-8 Classroom*. He can be found at www.billykrakower.com and on Twitter @wkrakower.

Jerry Blumengarten, also known as Cybrary Man, is a constant learner who is a champion of front-line educators who do their best to facilitate the learning of all students. Jerry taught for 32 years in the New York City school system. He can be found at www.cybraryman.com and on Twitter @cybraryman1.

Connecting Your Students with the Virtual World

Tools and Projects to Make Collaboration Come Alive

Second Edition

Billy Krakower
Jerry Blumengarten

Routledge
Taylor & Francis Group

NEW YORK AND LONDON

Second edition published 2021
by Routledge
52 Vanderbilt Avenue, New York, NY 10017

and by Routledge
2 Park Square, Milton Park, Abingdon, Oxon, OX14 4RN

Routledge is an imprint of the Taylor & Francis Group, an informa business

First edition published by Routledge 2015

Library of Congress Cataloging-in-Publication Data
A catalog record for this book has been requested

ISBN: 978-0-367-55948-9 (hbk)
ISBN: 978-0-367-55947-2 (pbk)
ISBN: 978-1-003-09580-4 (ebk)

Typeset in Palatino
by Apex CoVantage, LLC

Visit the eResources: www.routledge.com/9780367559472

Dedication

Billy:

To my wonderful wife, Jennifer, who has been there for me during the writing of both these editions of the book. You are my sounding board and supporter. Thank you for always taking care of our daughter Brianna when I need time to work on one of my projects.

Jerry:

To my beloved wife, Gail, who I miss so much and my children, Neil and Shira; son-in-law, Brad; my grandchildren Madison, Sam, Olivia, Jackson, and Ada; and my awesome global PLN, who inspire me every day.

To Paula:

Thank you for helping us with the first edition. Without your collaboration, this book would not exist.

Contents

eResources

A hyperlinked list of the online resources mentioned in this book is available on our website. To download, go to the book product page, www.routledge.com/9780367559472. Then click on the "eResources" tab and select the file. The document will begin downloading to your device. For the second edition, we will be posting the standards that we feel are relevant to the eResources. As standards are always changing, we feel that this is the easiest way to stay relevant.

Meet the Authors

Billy Krakower (@wkrakower) has been an educator in the classroom for over 14 years. Billy has spoken at various national and regional events including Empower19, Empower18, Empower17, ASCD16, the National Principals Conference 2017, ISTE 2019, ISTE 2015, ISTE2014, New Jersey Association of School Administrators, Techspo, New Jersey Association of Educational Technology Annual Conference, Edscape, NJEA, and Teacher Conference, among others. Although Billy speaks on a variety of topics and issues, common ones include: Connecting Beyond the Classroom, Twitter & You, Tech Tools to Use for the PARCC, Google Hangouts, Edmodo, and The Science Behind a Mystery Location Call. Billy is a Certified Google Trainer and ISTE Certified Educator.

Billy is also one of the co-moderators of #satchat (School Leaders) chats on Twitter. Billy is a 2014 ASCD Emerging Leader and a member of the NJASCD Executive Board, where he serves as the Technology Committee Chair. As an author, Billy has co-written five books, *Connecting Your Students with The World*, *Using Technology to Engage Students with Learning Disabilities*, *140 Twitter Tips for Educators*, *Hacking Google for Education*, and *Getting Started with STEAM: Practical Strategies for the K–8 Classroom*.

He is the Chief Financial and Event Officer for Evolving Educators, LLC (www.evolvingeducators.com).

Billy has an Advanced Certificate in Instructional, Design and Deliver, Educational Leadership and a dual master's degree in Special Education and Elementary Education from Long Island University. You can read more about Billy, his awards, and his presentations at www.billykrakower.com. He is passionate about helping every child and adult enjoy and learn using technology tools in easy, fun, and empowering ways.

Jerry Blumengarten (@cybraryman1), also known as Cybrary Man, is a constant learner who is a champion of front-line educators who do their best to facilitate the learning of all students. He considers himself a Twitterbrarian who is attempting to curate the Internet for educators, students, and parents. Jerry joyfully served as a moderator on #edchat. He has guest-moderated many other Twitter educational chats and created #engsschat. He has been a featured speaker at #METC13 and #GaETC13 was the keynote speaker at Tomorrow's Classrooms Today and gave keynote presentations at 15 Edcamps and TeachMeets. At ISTE he has given workshops and presentations and served on panels. He also is a commentator on BAM Radio.

Jerry taught for 32 years in the New York City school system. He worked in four inner-city middle schools in Brooklyn, for the first 20 years mainly as a social studies teacher, but he taught most subject areas and for the final 12 years he served as a teacher-librarian. He also helped coach two different schools to back-to-back city track championships. He wrote curriculum for his school district, the New York City Board of Education, and Open Doors, a school-business partnership. He also wrote over 35 booklets on the environment, safety, careers, and water, electrical, and gas safety for the Culver Company, a leader in supplying educational materials for the utility industry. He served on the executive board of the Association of Teachers of Social Studies, was very active in the National Council for the Social Studies (NCSS) presenting sessions, and served as chairperson of the Urban Social Studies Education Committee.

The middle school library site he created has morphed into Cybrary Man's Educational Web Sites, which has information on most subject areas for all grade levels. Jerry was a pioneer in the use of technology during his school career.

While living on Long Island he was elected several times to the town's library board. On Cape Cod he was elected as a charter commissioner and helped write a town charter that was approved. Jerry has his BA degree with a major in Political Science from the University of Pittsburgh and an MA degree in the Teaching of Social Studies from Hunter College, City University of New York.

Acknowledgments

The genesis of the first edition of this book came from the fact that we are connected educators who passionately see the need to connect our students to collaborate with the world. Paula, Billy, and Jerry originally got together as a result of their activity on Twitter. It took a few years, but we met each other at educational conferences. On Twitter we came together on #4thchat and started a weekly Google Hangout to generate ideas on ways to connect classes and collaborate. We would especially like to thank our Sunday Night Google Hangout group: Jessica Bamberger, Nancy Carroll, Dan Curcio, Kim Powell, and Jennifer Regruth.

We would like to thank the following people as well: Meghan Everette, Kate Baker, Shelly Sanchez Terrell, Natalie Franzi, Steve Isaacs, Chris Aviles, Heidi Samuelson, Mark Nechanicky, Krista Ray, and Lisa Scumpieru for your contributions to the book.

How to Use This Book

This book is meant to be used as a practical guide for connecting students to the virtual world. We, as educators, want you to be able to use this book as a how-to guide and refer to it for ideas and ways to connect. It is our hope that you will take advantage of the amazing collaborative tools that are available in the digital age to facilitate children's learning. We have used our own experiences, as well as those of many other teachers who have successfully connected their students using this method. Please feel free to adapt the ideas we have given you to suit your own students and classrooms. We hope that you find this book a valuable resource as you start connecting your students to collaborate with the world.

This book contains many different projects and ideas; all of these projects can meet Common Core Standards, ISTE, and Next Generation Standards. If you visit www.routledge.com/9780367559472 you can find a guide for the projects that align with the standards. We felt that it was important to take the correlation chart out of the book and move it to the website as standards are always changing and we want to provide the most up to date information. Please note that the **bold-faced** words (the first time they appear in the book) can be found in the glossary.

Five years later, video conferencing has changed!

When we discuss the phrase "connected classrooms," we mean that classrooms are connecting via video conferencing, GSuite, Office 365, Edmodo, or other platforms. However, almost all of these projects can be done in school without having to connect online. We know that educators might have limited technology and may not be able to connect with other classrooms as we have described in some of these projects. Keep in mind you can adapt these projects to make them work for your classroom. You do not always have to connect with another classroom via video conferencing; you can connect with the classroom across or down the hall. These projects can all be adapted to meet the technology available for your class, school, and district.

1

Connecting Your Students in 2021 and Beyond

Be Connected—Be Engaged—Be Informed

Many of today's classroom teachers know the importance of being **connected educators** and the fact that we should be modeling for our students how to become connected and be responsible global citizens. It is necessary, however, to have more of our teacher colleagues connected so that they can network with passionate educators all around the world. This will better facilitate the learning of the children we serve. We have grown as educators through our presence on **Twitter**. We have built strong global **PLN**s (personal or professional learning networks) that have enabled us to connect, share, and learn with passionate teachers, administrators, community members, and parents, as well as others interested in education. It has also provided us with the opportunity to connect our students with the world. With our students, however, we struggle to try to make these connections while covering the standards and preparing our students for the myriad of testing that is commonplace in most schools today. How can we fit it all together and make it work?

We will describe how the projects contained in our book can cover a multitude of standards, enabling today's teachers to weave it all together in a way that is engaging, fun, and meaningful for our students as they prepare for their global futures.

In the "dark ages" of the 1950s and 1960s, we reached out to others outside our classrooms via telephones whose lines were connected to wall outlets and by mailing letters. The picture-postcard exchanges decorated bulletin boards and allowed us to correspond with the world outside the classroom walls. The 1970s and 1980s saw the beginning of the use of online message boards to communicate. The **Email Around the World** project in the late 1990s produced wonderful exchanges from faraway places (www.cybrary-man.com/email.html). The **Flat Stanley** exchange began late in the 1990s and early 2000s and allowed classes to connect with one another via mail. However, what was lacking was a more personalized, "in the moment" exchange.

Connecting the Old-Fashioned Way

It is wonderful that technology enables us to connect easily and in the moment without having to wait. After the tech connection, though, it is nice to continue by resorting to the tried-and-true, old-fashioned ways of communicating. Having your students write personal letters and then sending them would be special. A couple of years ago Jerry's oldest grandson said it was not fair that his sisters got mail and he did not. He was right; we have lost this special way of communicating that is personal. Save copies of the letters your students write. Create a bulletin board showing copies of the students' letters and the responses they received. In some cases, companies send brochures and literature that really enhance the bulletin board.

Emailing

Once you have made a connection with another class, it is a good idea to maintain and build on the relationship formed to collaborate on other projects. One way to continue the connection is by using email. In 1999–2000, Jerry participated in an Email Around the World project. It was a fantastic way to connect with students all across the globe. It was long before the ability existed to connect in person via Skype or Google Meet or other such tools. Jerry made a great bulletin board (see Figure 1.1), which had a map of the world with the email responses showing where the connections originated. The actual email was connected by yarn to the country on the map where it originated. To see all of the emails that Jerry's classes received in their 1999 Email Around the World project, visit www.angelfire.com/stars3/education/emailworld.html.

Today with the available technology, we can easily connect our students almost instantaneously to classrooms around the world. We believe all classroom teachers should flatten the walls of their classroom to communicate, collaborate, and create with other classrooms around the globe and with experts in the different fields about which the students are studying. Using the myriad of web tools accessible to them, teachers should be reaching out

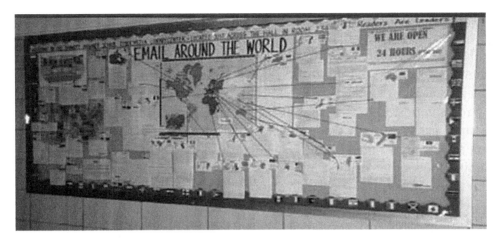

Figure 1.1 Email Around the World Project

as often as possible to help their students build and strengthen their global connections and add to their personal learning networks.

We feel that it is extremely important when working with your students to connect with them at first and show them that you really care. You should follow this natural progression of teaching connections, starting small and building up to bigger connections. After teacher-to-student relationships are solidified, it is important that students connect with their peers in the classroom and build a sharing, caring community.

A very important first step is working with your students toward being a good citizen in our digital world. We cannot stress enough the importance of **digital citizenship**. Please periodically review with your students how to be responsible users of technology. Explain the need to be careful about what they post online. Children have to be conscious of their digital presence and the **digital footprint** that they are creating. Talk to them about proper **netiquette** when they are connecting online. Please also communicate with their parents and make sure they understand the importance of parents keeping track of what their children are doing online.

The next step is to connect your class with other grade levels and experts outside the classroom. Students should be able to get answers to their questions from experts. You can then connect your students with other classes around the country and the world to learn and share with one another. The initial connections can lead to future collaborations.

The question always asked is, "How do I connect my students to other classes around the country or the world?" This is a major concern among all grade levels. There are many different **social media** venues in which we can connect in today's world—Twitter, **Edmodo**, Facebook, Instagram, and **Voxer**, just to name a few. There are groups available for any grade and any subject. Twitter, Facebook, and

Instagram have communities that allow educators to connect to the grade level, or subject area they teach. It is important to remember to use the # when searching for the communities or searching for posts. Some examples of # are #engchat (English), #sschat (social studies), #historyteacher, #Langchat (foreign language), #Literacy, #Math, #Mathchat, #MusEdchat (music), and #PhysEd.

You can post to the appropriate grade level or subject area you are teaching and search through the community for specific resources. When you are looking to connect on a project, be sure to use the # so everyone in the community knows that you are interested in participating in your project. Twitter, Facebook, and Instagram have communities that are an easy way to get started becoming a connected educator.

Another good way to connect is to join communities on Edmodo.[1] We recommend that you sign up for a free Edmodo account to take advantage of all it has to offer. Communities on Edmodo contain the main subject areas of language arts, math, science, and social studies, along with other communities including creative art, health and physical education, and special education. You can post or filter through these communities to find information or other educators to connect with around the world.

Twitter is another great way in which to connect with educators from across the world, and we have found it to be one of the best ways to become a connected educator. Twitter allows educators the ability to find many projects they can use in their classrooms. There are chats for most subject areas and grade levels. The schedule for **Twitter educational chats** can be found at bit.ly/educhatcalendar. Twitter is an easy way to connect with other educators or find a partner to do a project with. It is just a matter of using the appropriate **hashtag (#)** in order to find someone.

What is a hashtag? It is Twitter's way of aggregating tweets about a common topic into searchable data. For example, if you were looking for information about the Daily Five and teaching fourth grade you can tweet: "Looking for information on the #DailyFive **#4thchat**." Anyone who follows those hashtags will see the tweet come across on their timeline and could either respond to it or retweet it to others who might have a better knowledge of the subject. Another example would be if you were a middle school teacher teaching English and were about to start a study group on *The Hunger Games*; you might tweet, "Starting a book study on The Hunger Games. Anyone have any information? #mschat #engchat #edchat."

We have found that an easy entry point to making connections at the elementary level is through Mystery Location Calls using **Skype** or **Google Meet**. In Chapter 3, we will explain in depth how to get started with Mystery Location Calls. Participating in a Mystery Location Call is an engaging and tech-infused way to have students practice their geography and communication skills. During the calls, students are learning about other parts of the country or world through either inquiry or yes-or-no questions. Mystery

Locations Calls are fun and easy to run in your classroom. This book will examine ways in which to conduct a Mystery Location Call and explain the various jobs students have while conducting these calls. We will walk you step by step through the ins and outs of conducting a Mystery Location Call, starting with dividing your class into two groups to practice performing an actual Mystery Location Call. The step-by-step guide will give you the strategies that work best in the classroom.

What else is possible besides Mystery Location Calls? What can you do at different grade levels? We had discussed this point when we used to meet with our weekly Sunday night Google Hangout group, which consisted of teachers from seven different states who have done these calls with their classes. This book could not have been possible without the connections the authors have made with these wonderful educators. We have been working together over the last several years to come up with projects and activities to do as a follow-up to a Mystery Location Call or as an alternative to Mystery Location Calls. Through our connections on Twitter, Facebook, and Google+ (back when Google+ existed) and our own creativity, we have compiled a list of projects that teachers can move on to after they have begun collaborations through Mystery Location Calls.

These projects range from short, 20-minute activities to ones that can take place over several weeks. The chapters include other **video conferencing** ideas. We have provided suggested ways you can collaborate for all the seasons of the year. We have included a chart listing of all the projects. It is our hope that this book serves as a guide for ways to get involved with collaborative projects.

Fall and Winter Projects (Chapter 4)

September

Labor Day
September 11: Showing Compassion
Hispanic Heritage Month (September 15–October 15)
International Dot Day* (September 15)

October

LGBT History Month
Indigenous Peoples' Day
Fall—How Weather Affects Us*
Halloween Projects

November

Election Day
Veterans Day/Remembrance Day
Gettysburg Address*
Native American Heritage Month
Thanksgiving Day: Canada (October) vs. the United
States (November)
Plimoth Plantation*

December

Pearl Harbor Day
Sharing Different Holiday Celebrations

January

New Year's
Dr. Martin Luther King, Jr.*
Martin's Big Words*
100th Day of School*

February

American Heart Month*
Black History Month*
#K12Valentine Project
Lunar New Year
Groundhog Day
Super Bowl Connections*
Presidents' Day
The Winter Olympics

Spring and Summer Projects (Chapter 5)

March
Mardi Gras*
Read Across America—Dr. Seuss's Birthday*
Commonwealth Day
Pi Day—March 14 (3/14)
St. Patrick's Day*
Women's History Month

April

National Autism Awareness Month
Impromptu Calls*
Poetry Month*

Baseball
Holocaust Remembrance Day
Earth Day—Grocery Bag Project*
Arbor Day

May

National Inventors Month
10-Day Passion Challenge and Identity Day*
Cinco de Mayo (5th of May)*
Memorial Day

June

Flag Day
Graduation—End of School

*= The projects that we have participated in.

Connecting During School Closures

In the next few chapters, we will highlight tools and projects that can be used when school is in sessions and during school closures. In 2020 the way we approached education had drastically changed. However, we feel that this book is a great guide to be used when educators are in the classroom teaching students or when you are teaching in front of a computer. The projects in this book can be easily adapted to teach remotely with a few tweaks or be used while having students in a classroom. The world has changed, and in education, there may no longer be as many school closures. We hope this book serves as a blueprint on ways to connect your classroom or even a way to start new projects in your classroom. We hope you enjoy and find it useful!

Note

1. www.edmodo.com/about.

The Next Chapter

In Chapter 2 we will look at what video conferencing is, the benefits and disadvantages of video conferencing, and the importance of video conferencing.

2

Taking Video Conferencing to the Next Level

What Is Video Conferencing?

Video conferencing in schools has taken many different shapes over the past decade. In our experience circa 2016, video conferencing was mainly doing a Mystery Location Call, bringing in a guest speaker such as a scientist or an author, having a virtual debate with another class, or having a video chat with pen pals. The definition of video conferencing is "the holding of a conference among people at remote locations by means of transmitted audio and video signals," defined by Merriam-Webster. In education, video conferencing can look and take different shapes. Video conferencing is a valuable tool, especially during remote learning. It can be used to connect with your students and parents and to bring in guest speakers and connect classrooms in other schools. Perhaps we are in the future of video conferencing and we will be using this technique much more for instruction.

Fast forward to the 2020 school year, and how video conferencing in schools became the way students learned, teachers communicated, and meetings took place. The coronavirus pandemic changed the way most students were used to learning in school classrooms. The pandemic brought the necessity to use video conferencing for learning instruction. Students had access to the Internet and devices to carry out learning when students were sheltered in place. During the pandemic, teachers, students, parents, and experts were brought together with audio, video, and screen sharing features on any device wherever they were located. The future of video conferencing will change the landscape of education.

In this chapter, we will look at how video conferencing can be used inside the classroom to connect the students beyond the classroom walls to the world. We will discuss the benefits and disadvantages of using video conferencing in both school buildings and during remote learning. What are the different types of tools you can use for video conferencing, guides to help during calls, and ways to connect with authors and experts? According to John Hattie's research on visible learning, the effective size of technology with an effective size of elementary students is .44, and the use of online and digital tools has an effective size of .33 on student learning.[1] The research from John Hattie shows the importance of incorporating technology with students. Video conferencing is one of the many techniques that can have a positive effect on students.

Benefits and Uses of Video Conferencing

There are many benefits of video conferencing that include improving relationships, the flexibility of learning collaboration, and so much more. Communicating this way is more personal than phone calls, texts, or emails. The key is to use any device that you have in your classroom such as, **interactive whiteboard**, individual student laptops, tablets, or smartphones to conduct video conferences.

Video conferencing enables us now to connect with other classes all over the world easily. Commonalities and differences can be exchanged between different cultures and bring a better understanding of how each lives and learns. Educators can connect classrooms at all levels of education to provide epals or pen pals or even tutors. Imagine being able to connect older students with your students to help them learn and grow. Classrooms connect across school districts or across town who are not in the same school building. Video conferencing breaks down the walls and makes connections to be more accessible.

Connections between different levels of education can be very beneficial. Just think about the beauty of having a middle school student reading to a kindergartner or a high school student who wants to major in chemistry connecting with a college student in that major.

Enables Students to Record Lessons for Later Review

The ability to record classes can be precious for students who miss school because of illness or other situations. Their learning would not be impeded as they can keep up with their classmates. Viewing lessons again can also help students understand the material that was covered and was not understandable at first. We have to be aware that not every student learns the same way, and some need more repetition and time to absorb what has been presented. According to John Hattie, visible learning replay has a positive effect of .54. As educators in a changing world, we need to think about other ways to use video instruction with students. Blended learning and flipped classroom have been buzz words for half a decade in education. Using video instruction with students can have a positive impact. The tools that many educators learned to use during the global pandemic can be employed and have a positive impact on education. A blended or flipped approach can allow students to view instructions and then apply what they have learned.

Improves Relationships

At times when you cannot connect in person, a video conference can help keep and improve relationships. Teachers can reach out with their pictures and smiles to cheer up anxious students. Seeing someone face-to-face is an excellent opportunity to observe their facial expressions and body language, which cannot be done by text or email. Teachers can connect with students individually in a live chat that makes it much more personal and meaningful. Video conferencing enables students to connect to collaborate and share information on a global level. They can have a better cultural understanding by communicating with students in other countries.

Makes Scheduling of Parents/Teacher Meetings Convenient

Keeping parents informed of their child's learning is extremely important. Video conferencing makes it possible to get teachers and busy parents together at a convenient time for both without the necessity of travel, loss of work time, and waiting.

Allows for Flexibility

Video conferences can be scheduled at any time and can be carried out with a computer or a cell phone. Asynchronous learning can occur; sessions can be recorded and viewed at more convenient times for those who cannot make the actual broadcast. There is the ability to mute and unmute people, so it prevents cacophony from taking place. There is also the opportunity to work collaboratively on documents through the ability to share screens.

Makes Out-of-the-Class Learning More Convenient and Easier

Out of the class, learning can easily be accomplished with video conferencing. Most computers are now equipped with cameras. Learning from home is convenient and can be done at any time. Students can collaborate and work in groups or on their own. Students living far from schools, especially in rural areas, can still be connected to their teachers and school. In inclement weather, students can still attend school remotely without leaving their homes in storms, no matter where they live. Students facing long term health issues can continue their learning via video conferencing as well. We also need to remember that not all students and educators have the same access to the Internet. Local school districts need to work to make sure all students and staff members have access to a device and Internet when discussing remote learning. Video conferencing is a great concept, but not everyone can benefit from video conferencing if the right access is not provided.

Facilitates Virtual Field Trips—No Traveling Required

Video conferencing can alleviate the expense and time needed for actual field trips while still giving the students the benefits of learning. You can take your students anywhere in the world to learn from your classroom or home. Virtual field trips can not only take you around the world but back in time and to outer space. In Chapter 6, we explore many different types of virtual field trips that can take place.

Makes it Easier to Connect With Experts

Bringing in an expert remotely into your classroom can enhance your students' learning. Someone working in the field that your students are studying can bring their first-hand experience and ability to answer your students' questions. Billy loves to bring in experts when he can to his classrooms. Through the years, Billy has brought in scientists through Skype A Scientist (www.skypeascientist.com/). One project Billy remembers particularly well is when his students were working on the ExploraVision Project, and Billy was able to bring in an expert in the field of robotics.

Many different authors will do a video conference call with your classroom. Some of the authors do charge, and some do not charge. During World Read Aloud Day on February 5, 2020, Billy was able to have author Artemis Roehrig read her new book, *Does a Fiddler Crab Fiddle?*, to his second grade students, and they were able to ask the author questions during the video call. Connecting with authors is one easy way to do video conferencing with your students. In the past, Jerry has even done video conferencing calls with students.

Practical Examples

Video Conferencing With the Olympic Village

During the 2014 Winter Olympics, Jennifer Regruth's classroom was able to connect with a gold medal winner in bobsledding live from the athlete's village in Sochi, Russia. Several classes joined together in a Google Hangout (GHO) for this historic live video chat. With classes from Pennsylvania, California, Oregon, Michigan, Indiana, and New York, students heard first-hand about the village for the athletes, competition, food in the cafeteria, and what an honor it is to compete for the USA. One of the kids even asked if the athletes played tricks on each other!

A few days later, the classes watched live as Meryl Davis and Charlie White won their gold medals in ice dancing. Then in early May, Jennifer's class had a live chat with them. The class made signs and chanted, "USA!" The Olympians showed their gold medals, and the students were able to ask questions about their experience. Using technology to connect "face to face" and in groups is a game changer.

Read Alouds for Students

Read alouds are essential for students to hear during the day at school. However, when you are not in school, it can become difficult for students to hear a read aloud. During the pandemic, read alouds became even more critical as students were losing the vital time of hearing stories from their teachers. Video conferencing is a way to provide those read alouds to students. Tom Murray shared on Twitter that her daughter's teacher would invite her class for a bedtime story (Figure 2.1).

"She openly invited her class for an optional bedtime story. She gave them a few minutes to say hi to each other, greeted each one as mentioned. Called

Thomas C. Murray ✔
@thomascmurray

My son's kindergarten teacher is doing an optional bedtime story tonight. She's saying hi to every child as they log in and how she misses them.

Teachers really are some of THE BEST people on the planet. For those of you in the trenches every day... THANK YOU. 🤍

7:04 PM · Apr 15, 2020 from Pennsylvania, USA · Twitter for iPhone

Figure 2.1 Tweet From Thomas C. Murray About Bedtime Stories

their attention, read the bedtime story, and then gave them a few minutes to talk and connect," said Murray.

Billy's daughter is four years old, and even though Billy and his wife read to her every night, she was missing out on storytime at her pre-kindergarten program. An online program that Billy's wife found, My Fairy Tale Princess, would read stories to a child once a week. You had to sign up for the reading on Facebook, but it was an easy way for his daughter to hear stories. The person who was reading the story even dressed up as a princess. Authors of children's books were also offering read alouds during the pandemic. Read alouds are important to have in a child's life, and videos allow for read alouds to occur anytime. In January of 2020, Billy's school participated in One School One Book. The teachers and administrators in his school building all recorded themselves reading a chapter a day for the students to follow at home. The videos were released at the end of the school day, and students were surprised each day with a different guest reader. To learn more about the One School One Book, check out https://readtothem.org/programs/one-school-one-book/.

Disadvantages of Video Conferencing

Disadvantages could include a lack of personalization, cost, training, time zones, network instability, and time lag. Sometimes during video conferencing the video might freeze; a delay or lag could take place; or you might experience unstable audio, blurry images, or the inability to screen share. Your connection might not be good. You may need to check the Internet connection speed and bandwidth. There are instances where attendees have to be muted so it does not interfere with the session.

There are often technical issues along with making sure you are getting all users on the same page at the same place. You might inevitably encounter technical difficulties when video conferencing. These problems might be caused by network failure, hardware, or software issues. You should anticipate such problems and be prepared with technical support. Structure is vital in teaching when you are video conferencing with students. It, at times, can seem less structured and organized. There is a need for planning before you conduct a video conference. There is a great benefit to learning if there are organization and structure. One major problem is to make sure all participants are on the same page.

Expenses associated with subscriptions and equipment can also be a disadvantage in video conferencing. Costs to have video conferencing vary according to what platform your school adopts and your needs.

You have to consider factors like the cost of subscription, calls, equipment, licensing fees, costs of calls, the bandwidth necessary, set up, and troubleshooting. You should have a security system that will not be compromised. You also have to factor in the training of staff and maintenance of the equipment.

Time Zone Differences

Connecting your students with others around the world creates the necessity to deal with time zones. In some cases, connections cannot be met during school times. It is essential to set a reasonable time for both parties to communicate, making sure you connect with the person with whom you will be speaking before the video conference to discuss the times. Double-check to make sure that you are both talking about the same time zone and add EST at the end if you are on the East Coast, or add the designation for whichever time zone you are in.

Lack of Personalization

Many see the use of technology as losing the human connection. Personal interaction enables a better observation of facial expressions and body language. The handshake or hug (before coronavirus) enhances a personal connection that cannot be done with video. Poor audio or visuals cannot replace a meeting face to face.

Cybersecurity and Privacy Issues

Unfortunately, if the networks and tools you are using are not secure, you are open to being hacked, which means having an outside source obtain your information or interfere with what you are doing without permission. Your audio/video communication and student privacy must be protected. Parents need to be notified of how they are securing student privacy and can have their child opt-out of that form of communication. You also want to protect the identity of your students by not using their surnames.

Video Conferencing Applications

There are so many different tools to use in education for video conferencing. Depending on the school district, some of these tools are allowed and not allowed to be used. Make sure you always check with the district administration before using the tools. These tools are always changing, and there are always new updates coming out. For example, Google Meet has been making improvements during the pandemic based on user feedback. Below we give a quick description of each tool and a website to find out more information about the tools.

Google Meet

"Multi-person video calls are a breeze as you reach your students wherever they are. With Google Meet, you can store files and find what you need instantly and manage users, devices, and data securely and efficiently."

Google Meet: https://gsuite.google.com/products/meet/
Jerry's Google Meet page: http://cybraryman.com/googlehangout.html

Zoom

"Simplified video conferencing with real-time messaging and content sharing across any device. **Zoom** helps schools improve student outcomes with secure video communication services for hybrid classrooms, office hours, administrative meetings, and more."

Zoom's Page: https://zoom.us/
Jerry's Zoom page: www.cybraryman.com/zoom.html

Skype

"Host a video or an audio conference with up to 50 people, record your calls, enable live captions and subtitles, or simply talk over smart chat. Skype makes it easy to stay in touch."

Skype Page: www.skype.com/en/

Microsoft Teams

"Work remotely without feeling remote. **Microsoft Teams** enables you to go instantly from a group chat to a video conference. You can have as many people as possible meeting in one place, no matter where they are located. You can also share and edit Word docs, PowerPoint, and Excel files in real-time."

Teams Page: https://products.office.com/en-us/microsoft-teams/group-chat-software

Seesaw

"Students use built-in annotation tools to capture what they know in Seesaw's digital portfolio. Teachers deeply understand student thinking and progress—enabling them to teach better. Families gain a window into their student's learning and engage with school happenings."

Seesaw page: https://web.seesaw.me/
Jerry's Seesaw page: http://cybraryman.com/seesaw.html

Alternatives

◆ BlueJeans
◆ CISCO Webex Meetings
◆ ClickMeeting
◆ Free Conference
◆ GoToMeeting
◆ Intermedia Unite
◆ Jitsi

Etiquette and Privacy Guide for Students

Based on the "Video Conferencing Tools in the Age of Remote Learning: Privacy Considerations for New Technologies" that COSN has developed, we thought these were two key questions to consider:

◆ "Even if you are using a designated school account, review the privacy policy and terms as you would for any other technology. If you need the provider to sign a data protection agreement, do so. The COVID-19 crisis does not mean cutting corners on privacy. Just the opposite. Give yourself and your parent community the comfort you both need to know that the tools you are using are appropriate for your students and compliant with the laws.

◆ To further protect student data privacy, avoid setting up a video conference system that requires students to create accounts. Remember that accounts for these systems are often intended only for adults. Instead, create an enterprise account for your school system and give teachers access. Accounts should be configured so no student user can create their own account unless the required data sharing can be done in compliance with all the applicable laws and account sign-ins necessary for safety reasons. Otherwise, students should be able to join the classroom via a simple web link provided by the teacher."[2]

Etiquette is important to teach students when using video conferencing, especially where there are different features between Google Meet, Zoom, Skype, and Teams. During the time of writing this book, Billy had developed a guide for Google Meet, and through his PLN, one was developed for Zoom by Lisa Scumpieru (Figure 2.2).

Figure 2.2 Zoom Guide on Video Conferencing Etiquette

Google Meet Etiquette Guide for Students

These are just a few suggested ideas (Figure 2.3). As Google is always making updates and changes to Meet, we wanted to give you a general idea of strategies to use. Please visit www.routledge.com/9780367559472 to get an update chart and a printable chart.

Figure 2.3 Google Meet Etiquette Guide for Students

◆ When you enter the Meet/Hangout, mute yourself (if you are already not muted).

◆ When you have a question, type it in the textbox and wait for your teacher to call on you.

◆ When you have something to contribute to what is being said, but it is not your turn, use the chat feature in the right-hand corner or use the raise your hand feature.

- Wait for the teacher to call on you to unmute yourself.
- Only one student should contribute/talk at a time.
- Look into the camera when you are talking.
- Stay attentive. Pay attention to your teacher or other students who are speaking.
- Remember, you are on camera and should be dressed appropriately.

Make sure to check out Jerry's page on etiquette, netiquette, and social skills: https://cybraryman.com/etiquette.html.

A few helpful tips on video conferencing:

- Make sure you always wear headphones.
- Do a microphone check.
- Do a video camera check.
- Check out lighting, such as a ring light, as it can help make you more visible in the video.

Conclusion

It is essential to examine all the benefits and disadvantages of video conferencing in schools and make your decision based on how your staff, students, and parents feel about it. You have to take into consideration that not all students learn the same way. This would be another possible learning avenue for students who could benefit from it. Keep it simple, as video conferencing can get overwhelming quickly.

Those presenting the video conference need to be thoroughly familiar with the system and ready to troubleshoot if necessary. The viewers should receive a tutorial on how to video conference, proper etiquette instructions, and a FAQ list if they encounter audio, visual, or other connection problems. Remember, there is so much information on video conferencing that we hope that this chapter serves as a starting point for you to get started with video conferencing in the classroom.

Notes

1. "Global Research Database." Corwin Visible Learning Plus. www.visible learningmetax.com/Influences.
2. *Video Conferencing Tools in the Age of Remote Learning: Privacy Considerations for New Technologies*. 2020, Video Conferencing Tools in the Age of Remote

Learning: Privacy Considerations for New Technologies. www.cosn.org/sites/default/files/Member%20Brief%20-%20Video%20Conferencing%20040120.pdf

Resources

20 Ideas for Video Conferencing With Students | Infused Classroom @Holly ClarkEdu: www.hollyclark.org/2020/04/21/video-conference-ideas/
Tips and Tools for Teaching Remotely @rmybrne: www.freetech4teachers.com/2020/03/tips-and-tools-for-teaching-remotely.html

The Next Chapter

In Chapter 3, we will go step-by-step through planning Mystery Location Calls with your students.

3

The Practical Guide to a Mystery Location Call 2.0

What is a Mystery Location Call? A Mystery Location Call is an exciting, engaging educational guessing game played by two or more classes. The classes connect using a video conferencing platform such as Skype or Google Meet to figure out where the other class or classes are located. If this is not done with a predetermined game plan, it could take quite a long time. From others who pioneered these calls and through our own experiences, we have learned a great deal about how to make these calls very successful and captivating experiences for all the students involved. We are going to take you through those steps so that you too can use Mystery Location Calls to start connecting your students with others. We have also discovered that starting with Mystery Location Calls as your first foray into connecting leads to future collaborations with the teachers and classrooms you meet during your calls. A Mystery Location Call addresses the twenty-first-century skills known as the **Four Cs (4Cs)**—collaboration, communication, creativity, and critical thinking. On top of that, this learning adventure is so much fun and so engaging to your students that they will be begging for more.

Mystery Location Calls:

- ◆ Inner Workings of a Mystery Location Call
- ◆ Preparing Students for Mystery Location Calls
- ◆ Supplies for a Mystery Location Call
- ◆ Finding People for a Call
- ◆ Overcoming Different Time Zones to Connect With the World

- ◆ Jobs for Students
- ◆ Skills Developed by Students Participating in Mystery Location Calls
- ◆ Sample Inquiry-Based Questions
- ◆ Sample Yes-or-No Questions
- ◆ Practicing a Mystery Location Call
- ◆ After the Call—Making It a Learning Experience
- ◆ Writing a Blog
- ◆ What to Do After the First Mystery Location Call to Continue the Connections

Inner Workings of a Mystery Location Call

There are some very important parts of the Mystery Location Call that have to take place to ensure a successful connection. Communication with the other teacher(s) is crucial. All involved teachers have to know how the call will work. Running a test of the conferencing tool (Skype, Google Meet, etc.) is important. Check the visual and audio parts and see if they are working well. Make sure everyone knows about the time constraints as a typical call lasts about 20 minutes. Discuss the type of questions that the students will prepare. There are typically two different types of questions that people like to use: inquiry-based questions and yes-or-no questions. Examples of both of these types of questions appear later in this chapter.

Occasionally students will quickly be able to discover the state where the other class is located. To keep the call going, you could have the class try to also figure out the city where the other class is located. The students have to really think and become great researchers in order to correctly guess the city, but it does work and it is fun to watch students in this challenge. We will provide sample questions to help guide you through this part as well.

Preparing Students for Mystery Location Calls

The teacher needs to explain how a Mystery Location Call works. We suggest watching some **YouTube** videos of other classes that have participated in these calls. While watching these videos, students should keep track of what they liked and did not like, as well as ideas about how to improve those calls. To motivate your students, show them the Super Bowl ad for Microsoft featuring an Irvine, California, classroom doing a Mystery Location Call.[1] Have your students practice communication skills with and without technology—listening, speaking (enunciating, pace, tone, volume)—and be aware of **body language**, including eye contact and **microexpressions**. Have your students view the video of the practice call so they can watch and listen to themselves to find ways they can improve their body language and speech.

The teacher might want to set up a reminder using the **Remind** app to keep the students and parents up to date on the upcoming Mystery Location Call and what needs to be done.

Before the actual call, it is necessary to have your students do research on their state and city and start coming up with clues to be used during the call. You can group the clues into easy, medium, or hard. Have the class vote on which clues to use.

In the past Billy had his students complete a project, a **PowerPoint**, on New Jersey and their city. The goal is that the students have prior knowledge about the state and city before doing Mystery Location Calls that involve inquiry-based questions. The students should be able to answer questions similar to those that will be used during a call. Some of the questions are as follows:

- In what region of the United States is our state located?
- What is the capital of our state?
- Name two rivers that flow through our state.
- Name three famous people from our state and tell why they are famous.
- What are some products that our state is known for?
- List two to four famous landmarks found in our state.
- What is our state flower?
- What is our state bird?
- In what time zone are we located?
- What kind of animals do we find in our state?
- Name two states that border our state.

Supplies for a Mystery Location Call

Before starting a Mystery Location Call, it is important to have certain supplies available in order to help make the call easier. The following supplies are recommended: a computer that connects to the Internet with a **webcam** (this is a necessity), microphones, maps of the United States or the world, pencils, erasers, scrap paper, computers for students, clipboards, photo camera, video camera, and clocks showing different times zones. There are many sources from which to obtain free or inexpensive supplies and equipment for your class, including these major sources: DonorsChoose, Digital Wish, Adopt a Classroom, and ClassWish. We highly recommend letting your parent-teacher organization, parents of your students, and businesses in your community know about your needs. You can also write a grant to obtain the items you need.

Billy uses the following setup when he does his calls: a Yeti Microphone and a Microsoft Lifecam on a tripod, which works great, and a USB extender. (Please note that the webcam he uses is not compatible with an Apple computer.)

Finding People for a Call

There are many ways that you can find teachers willing to do a Mystery Location Call with your class. Social media has made it much easier to find other classes with which to conduct Mystery Location Calls and other collaborative activities. Twitter has flattened the world and provided a great way to connect with teachers all over the world. Different grade-specific Twitter Chats have produced lists of teachers willing to do Mystery Location Calls. Skype has a website where you can find other classrooms and connect as well. Skype has called them Mystery Skype calls, but it is the same idea as a Mystery Location Call (https://education.skype.com/).

Overcoming Different Time Zones to Connect With the World

In order to connect classes from all over the globe, it is necessary to be creative. You may have to pre-record sessions and questions. If you cannot connect because of time zone issues, have your students come up with a Mystery Location Scavenger Hunt for the other class to use to find your location. Open school evenings or family event nights also provide chances to connect. Enlist the school librarian to help carry out these connections with students attending the parent-teacher evening sessions.

There is a convenient way to connect with other classrooms in various time zones. Skype in the Classroom has a #MysterySkype page where you can find contacts by location and age group.[2]

Jobs for Students

To have a successful and engaging experience, each student in the class should have a function during a Mystery Location Call. Practicing will ensure a successful call. Divide the class into two groups and go through a trial call in class without using a connecting tool. Please film this practice call so that the entire class can review it to see how they functioned. Have each group secretly pick a different state than the one they live in. Make sure the students know exactly what their jobs entail. Tell the students that during future calls the jobs will be rotated. Also keep in mind our jobs list is a suggestion. Feel free to add to or subtract from this list as needed. Just remember that for the most successful experience during Mystery Location Calls, each student needs to be actively engaged.

The following is a description of jobs that you can employ with your students. Select the ones that you and your students are most comfortable with using. Depending on your class size and their feelings, adjust the number of students for the jobs that you have selected. There is a lot of flexibility in the different jobs, allowing for classes of different sizes to adjust to meet the need of their classes.

Lead Student: The Lead Student is like the director of a movie who makes sure everything runs smoothly and jobs are being done well. This job entails troubleshooting problems that arise, keeping the call moving, and in dead spots inserting Entertainers to keep the call interesting. Have this student draw a diagram of the classroom and the location of all the jobs. The Lead Student can decide how many students are needed for each job and can install an assistant to help. Directly after the call, the Lead Student should start a Google Doc on things that need improvement. The Lead Student should then have the other students in the class add to the document. We suggest that one student handle this very important job.

Visual Arts Director: This job is equivalent to the person in charge of the scenery and props used on a movie set. This student should carefully watch a film of the classroom during the trial call to make the part of the classroom that will be seen on the video call looks good and does not give any clues to the actual location. The Visual Arts Director makes sure that there are necessary visual aids for the call. They have to ensure that there are signs for the class and name cards (only use given names) for Greeters, Questioners, and Answerers. We suggest one student handle this job.

Greeter: The Greeter is like the emcee; this person welcomes the other class in a fun way without revealing their location. This student needs excellent verbal and nonverbal communication skills. Sometimes this person can also end the call. This function can be combined with the Closer job. It is wise to have a name card with the student's given name only and have a banner of the class in the background. We suggest having one to two students for this job.

Question Developers (Researchers): The Question Developers are like script-writers. They design clever questions and provide the questions and their answers to the Question Reviewers. It is important that the teachers in the call discuss the type of questions (most calls use only yes-or-no questions) to be used during the call to make sure there is no confusion among the students. Students can develop a database of questions in different categories to assist in development of appropriate questions. Arrange this group near the Question Reviewers and Questioners. This job could have a number of students, anywhere from two to six depending on the size of the class.

Question Reviewers: They decide on the order of these questions. These students must listen closely to the interchange. They analyze the questions and answers from the Question Developers to make sure they follow what has taken place so far during the call. They have to be prepared to change the next question(s) as a result of what they hear. They can employ Runners, who take questions to the Questioner or, if allowed, text the question. Given that the previous job could have a number of students, we would suggest that this job could also have more than one student. Ideally you want to have at least two students doing this job, but you can have anywhere from two to six students depending on the size of the class. The overall idea is to always make sure every student has a job and is doing something during the call.

Questioners: The Questioners have to ask the questions in a clear voice that can be heard and easily understood. We suggest that you have a boy and a girl perform this job. They can alternate asking the questions. If you have a smaller class this job can be combined with the Greeters.

Answerers: These students need to brainstorm and come up with logical answers to the questions they are asked. Students can employ appropriate tech tools (graphic organizers, **spreadsheets**, **databases**, etc.) to help with their predictions and draw conclusions. They need to choose one member of the group to give the answer. We suggest as many as four students could be in this group.

Geographers: The Geographers have to quickly analyze the clues given by the opposing class. Using wall maps, atlases, or maps on computers, they have to narrow down the area to search. They work along with the Map Puzzlers. Place these two teams close to one another. We suggest that there be a few students for each team.

Map Puzzlers or Logical Reasoners: Map Puzzlers or Logical Reasoners remove states, cities, or countries that have been eliminated by clues that have been given. It is a good idea to have a jigsaw puzzle of the United States or the world, depending on the call. If you do not have puzzle maps and are only having Logical Reasoners, allow them to work with the Geographers to figure out where the call is coming from. We recommend three to five students for the job depending on your class size.

Runners: The Runners transfer information between the different jobs during the call. Make sure there is a clear path between the stations. If you have a **BYOD (Bring Your Own Device)** policy in place, you can have "runners" text the information between stations. We suggest between two and four students for this job.

Backchannelers: This job requires that your students have access to devices that are connected to the Internet. A **backchannel** is a digital conversation that happens at the same time as a face-to-face activity. While the Mystery Location Call is happening, students are on devices using web tools like TodaysMeet or an Edmodo group as their backchannel platform. They type what is being said during the Mystery Location Call and chat with students from the other location. It is very important that the backchannelers do not reveal any information while chatting that could give away their location. Determine ahead of time if the other class will have students who will be backchanneling, decide on the platform, and share the address to the TodaysMeet room or the code to the Edmodo group prior to the start of the call. The number of students who are assigned this job will depend on the number of devices you have access to. Four to five students is ideal.

Photographers/Videographers: The camera crew takes still images and a videotape of the call. It is important that schools have parental permission to post any videos or photos of students. Usually, permission for a Mystery Location Call is not needed if it is not being recorded. Double-check with your school's **Acceptable Use Policy** regarding recording and photographing students. There are also programs you can use if you need to blur out a student's face. The number of students for the Photographer/Videographer job depends on how many cameras you have access to and the number of students in the class. Create a multimedia presentation of the call when it is concluded. Make sure you have at least one to two students for this job, though the maximum number of students recommended is four.

Time Keeper: The Time Keeper keeps the Mystery Location Call going within the time limit, which is usually about 20 minutes. This student can utilize a computer countdown timer, watch, or clock and should hold up easily read time signs. The time signs indicating minutes left can be prepared in advance. He or she can also use a bell to indicate one minute left. We recommend only one student for this position.

Tech Help Squad: The student Tech Help Squad will be ready to trouble-shoot technology problems to help the teacher make sure the call works. They will ensure that students can be heard and seen. They are responsible for carrying out visual and sound checks before and during the call. The following jobs are part of this team: Sound Engineer, Visual Director, and Tech Trouble-shooter. We recommend at least three students.

Social Media Sharers: Decide on a special hashtag (#) for this event and have students report on the progress of the call on Twitter. You can also share pictures and stories on Facebook. Remember: if using social media, make sure you eliminate your location on your biography. One student would be perfect for this job. If you have a large class, consider using different types of social media, but it would be tough for multiple students to be using one Twitter account at a time.

Bloggers: These students are taking notes about the Mystery Location Call and will write a **blog** post about the experience. The blog post will be shared with the other classes to promote future connections and collaborations. The ideal number for this job is one or two students. This can also be a great writing experience for a whole class activity.

State Facts Sharers: Once the state or city of the class has been determined, have some students share some interesting facts about their state, city, and school. Some examples of things to share are famous people, interesting sights, products manufactured, or produce the state might be known for. Tell the other class about your school—its mascot, prominent graduates—and some fun facts about your community. We suggest you have these students create a database or spreadsheet of these state facts. If time has run out, please share these facts with the other class by mail, either regular or electronic, or on a blog. This will continue the exchange between the classes.

Closers: The Closers end the call by thanking the other class for their participation in the call. After the location has been determined, the Closers can share interesting products from your state. For example, students in a school in Michigan displayed cereals produced in their state. Have the Closers prepared to open the door to future collaborations by inviting the other class to visit your blog or send emails, or encourage them to have a suggestion of a topic for a future video call. Ideas for a follow-up video call include surveying each other about favorite items and doing a presentation or a demonstration for the other class, which could include singing a song, reciting poetry, doing a science demo, or debating an interesting topic. The page www.cybraryman.com/states.html has a lot of information you can use. Ideally it would be nice to have one or two students as Closers.

These jobs are ones that we have found worked well or that have been successful with others in their classrooms. Keep in mind that the number of students for each job can vary according to your class size. Feel free to find what works best for your class since every classroom setting and environment is different.

Skills Developed by Students Participating in Mystery Location Calls

During these calls, students develop many different skills that are valuable in today's world. Reading and writing standards are addressed through these global projects by having the students work on collaborative **Google Docs**. In preparation for these calls the students perform myriad research skills. During the call they use online resources to research clues. Reading and writing skills are also addressed as the students can backchannel in a Google Doc, using Edmodo or TodaysMeet. They practice communication skills by speaking, listening, and engaging in nonverbal communication while participating in the video conferencing calls. After the video conference concludes, the students should blog or write about their experiences. They can also start communicating more with the other class via a safe, closed social learning network like Edmodo.

Teachers should model for their students how to work in our digital age. Teachers make global connections via Twitter, Facebook, Instagram, and other social media sites to enable their students to collaborate with other students around the globe.

A number of these skills fall under the "21st Century Student Outcomes and Support System" put out by the Partnership for 21st Century Skills.[3] Students develop and enhance their critical thinking and problem-solving skills during Mystery Location Calls. Students need to think quickly and use reasoning skills to answer the questions they are being asked. Since these calls are live, students also need to be able to use deductive reasoning skills at a moment's notice to solve the puzzle of where in the world the other class is located.

You may not at first think that creativity fits the concept of Mystery Location Calls; however, students are coming up with questions as well as asking them. They are brainstorming on their feet and being creative in how they ask questions along with the ways in which they are solving the location.

Today it is important for students to learn how to collaborate with one another. During Mystery Location Calls, teamwork skills are enhanced as the students work together to solve a mystery and solve problems. Students communicate and collaborate with a global audience via Skype or Google Meet as they participate in Mystery Location Calls. This leads to classrooms collaborating on other projects. They learn and model proper digital citizenship and communication skills as they ask and answer the clues that help them discover where the other class is located. One of the major twenty-first-century skills that a Mystery Location Call addresses is **collaboration**. Students collaborate and learn team building both with their classmates and with students outside of their classroom.

Another valuable skill used in these calls is time management. Since there is usually a limited amount of time for each call, the students have to use it wisely. Decision making not only goes along with time management but is also an important skill for students to learn early on. Students need to know how to make quick decisions and eliminate states in which the other class is not located. This leads us to another skill learned during a Mystery Location Call: **deductive reasoning**. Students have to deduce which states can be eliminated based on the information uncovered through each answered question.

Students are becoming globally aware of their surroundings. During Mystery Location Calls we are breaking down the walls of our classroom and showing students the world around them. It is important in today's world for students to become globally aware of other cultures and how we all look different but can become connected. Other proficiencies being taught are geography skills and research skills, both of which are very important to any learner and should be taught at all age levels.

Looking at all of the skills we come to realize how important it is to be digitally literate. We must make sure we are talking to students about **digital literacy** and how we are using digital skills during these calls. You should also be talking about the importance of being a good digital citizen.

Sample Inquiry-Based Questions

- How would you describe the weather now?
- Do you experience any extreme weather? If so, what kind?
- Do you live in an urban, suburban, or rural area?
- What time is it where you are right now? (This is a great question for students to gain an understanding of other time zones around the world.)
- What kind of agriculture products are grown in your state?
- What are some animals that you might see in the wild in your state?
- What are some famous places, tourist attractions, or popular events from your state?
- Who are some of the famous people born in your state?
- What is your state's nickname?

- Does your state border any bodies of water? If so, please name it.
- What region of the United States are you located in?
- Name one state that borders your state.
- What is the population of your state?
- What is something your state is famous for?
- What is your state's capital?

Once the students guess the state, if there is enough time left, have them try to determine the city the other class is located in. If you decide to end with just the state location, make sure you are prepared to share some information about your state and even your school and classroom.

- What is the name of your school?
- Where is your school located?
- How many students are in your school?
- What grades does your school include?
- Does your school have a mascot or motto?
- Briefly describe some things that you like about your school.
- What language do kids in your classroom speak other than English? What other languages are children fluent in?

Sample Yes-or-No Questions

- Are you in the United States?
- Are you (east/west) of the Mississippi River?
- Are you in the (Eastern, Central, Mountain, Pacific, etc.) time zone?
- Is your state in the (Northeast, Southeast, Southwest, Midwest, or West) region?
- Does your state border (Canada/Mexico)?
- Does your state border more than ___ states?
- Does your state have a coastline?
- Does your state border the (Atlantic/Pacific) Ocean or Gulf of Mexico?
- Is your state east of the Rocky Mountains?
- Does the ____ River flow through your state?
- Does your state's name have two words in it?
- Does the name of your state have a Native American origin?
- Does your state/country start with the letter ___?
- Is there a major river that borders your state?
- Is your state landlocked?

Practicing a Mystery Location Call

As we have stated before in the section "Jobs for Students," we suggest carrying out a practice call. Divide the class in half and have them select students for all the jobs. Let them decide on their mystery locations. Videotape the practice and go over with the entire class the good points and those that need to be improved. You could also try the call with another class in your school to make sure everything will run smoothly.

During the practice session have the photographers take pictures. Check the audio of your equipment and the students. The teacher should definitely connect with the other teacher on a Skype or Google Meet call to make sure the connection works and the audio is fine. Make students aware that they should not give away clues to their location. On the Mystery Location Call day do not wear any clothes that indicate your location; for example, clothing featuring professional sports teams usually show those from your state or city. Make sure students know the time period of the call. You need to keep within that time frame, so questions and answers have to be timed. Plan the time schedule with the other teacher beforehand.

After the Call—Making It a Learning Experience

So was this activity a learning experience? To find out, have each student complete an **exit slip** (see Figure 3.1 for an example) recording what they learned during the Mystery Location Call. This is a great formative assessment of their learning. They can include what worked and what did not work so you can make adjustments for your future Mystery Location Calls. Believe us when we say that your students will be begging for more of them.

3	Things I Learned Today . . .
2	Things I Found Interesting . . .
1	Questions I Still Have . . .

Figure 3.1 Example of an Exit Ticket

Writing a Blog

Writing a blog is a great way to have your students discuss their experience participating in a Mystery Location Call. Share the students' blog posts with the class they connected with and have them respond and comment. The blog posts can be shared with other classes as well. The use of the hashtag #comments4kids, created by William Chamberlain (@wmchamberlain), enables the children to get comments from people outside the walls of their classroom. Blogging gives even the quietest student a global voice.

What to Do After the First Mystery Location Call to Continue the Connections

Before you end your first Mystery Location Call, set a date and time to reconnect with this class. Before the next video call, each class will have the students create a series of survey questions that can be asked of the other class during the call. Have the classes take turns interviewing each other and gathering the answers to the survey questions. As your second call with this class is wrapping up, set another date and time to connect; each class then turns the previously collected data into graphs before sharing how your class's answers compare to their class's answers. Now one Mystery Location Call has been turned into three collaborative connections with the same group of students.

Notes

1. *Mystery Skype: Connecting Classrooms Around the World*, www.youtube.com/watch?v=GZdMnkWHG7s.
2. https://education.skype.com.
3. www.p21.org/our-work/p21-framework.

Resources

Four Cs: www.cybraryman.com/4cs.html
Geography: www.cybraryman.com/geography.html
Google Meet: www.cybraryman.com/googleMeet.html

ITM42, Mystery Location Calls video on YouTube: www.youtube.com/ watch?v=q0dpOXXMBMg

Mrs. Carroll's Classroom Blog: Mystery State Skype Preparation: www. mrscarroll310.blogspot.com/2012/09/mystery-state-skype-prepara tion.html

Ms. Naugle's Classroom Blog: Our First Mystery Location Call Using Google Hangout (Now Google Meet): www.pnaugle.blogspot. com/2012/10/our-first-mystery-state-google-hangout.html

Mystery Location Call: www.cybraryman.com/mysterylocationcall.html

Mystery Location Call Resources page—Billy Krakower: www.billykrakow er.com/mystery-location-call-resources-page.html

Powell4thGrade: Our Very First Mystery Skype This Year With Our New Friends in Ohio! www.powell4thgrade.blogspot.com/2011/10/our-very-first-mystery-skype-this-year.html

Regruth Hub: Our First Mystery Skype! www.brownroom18.blogspot. com/2013/08/our-first-mystery-skype.html

Remind: www.cybraryman.com/remind.html

Skype: www.cybraryman.com/skype.html

Skype in the Classroom: https://education.skype.com

The Next Chapter

Now that you have an understanding of the Mystery Location Call, in Chapter 4 we will share other ways you can connect and collaborate. We are going to present ideas to connect classes during the course of the school year in the forthcoming chapters. We are going to take a look at how to connect during different months of the year.

4

Fall and Winter Projects

As educators, we feel it is important that students understand different holidays and events that occur during the school year. In some cases, students get days off from school and do not really know why. In this and the next chapter we will show you ways to incorporate the seasons, holidays, events, and celebrations into your lessons and use them as a way to connect with other classes as well. As a reminder when we discuss the word "connected classrooms," we mean that classrooms are connecting via video conferencing, GSuite, Office 365, Edmodo or other platforms. However, almost all of these projects can be done in school without having to connect online. We know that educators might have limited technology and may not be able to connect with other classrooms as we have described in some of these projects. Keep in mind you can adapt these projects to make them work for your classroom. You do not always have to connect with another classroom via video conferencing; you can connect with the classroom across or down the hall. These projects can all be adapted to meet the technology available for your class, school, and district.

In this chapter we are going to explore different projects that we have either participated in or think would be great projects to connect a classroom. This chapter will cover projects during the fall and winter months. These projects usually occur during the months of September, October, November, December, January, and February. Depending on where you are located, some of these projects might be a good way to kick off becoming a connected classroom. We have also included ideas on how to celebrate holidays and events that occur during this season.

The winter season in our hemisphere lends itself to many ways to connect with classes all over the world to talk about the climate and weather conditions where they are located. Math and science activities can include movement of the Earth, temperature, wind chill, precipitation, composition of snow, amount of snow, lake-effect snow, polar vortex, and animals' hibernation and movement during winter. Compare the winter activities you enjoy doing with the activities of students in other areas of this country and around the world. What would be interesting is connecting with classes who have the opposite seasons. For example: the Australian seasons are opposite of those in the northern hemisphere.

This is meant to be a practical guide for finding projects that are useful and advice on different ways in which to start collaborating. These projects can be used as a follow-up to Mystery Location Calls or as separate projects that can be used to connect your students with other classrooms. The asterisk (*) indicates projects that we have participated in. If there is not an asterisk, these are ideas or suggestions that you could expand upon in your classroom.

Fall and Winter Projects

September	October	November
Labor Day	LGBT History Month	Election Day
September 11: Showing Compassion	Indigenous Peoples' Day	Veterans Day/Remembrance Day
Hispanic Heritage Month (September 15–October 15)	Fall—How Weather Affects Us*	Gettysburg Address*
International Dot Day* (September 15)	Halloween Projects	Native American Heritage Month
		Thanksgiving Day: Canada (October) vs. the United States (November)
		Plimoth Plantation*

December	January	February
Pearl Harbor Day	New Year's	American Heart Month*
Sharing Different Holiday Celebrations	Dr. Martin Luther King, Jr.*	Black History Month*
	Martin's Big Words*	#K12Valentine Project
	100th Day of School*	Lunar New Year
		Groundhog Day
		Super Bowl Connections*
		Presidents' Day
		The Winter Olympics

September Projects

Labor Day

The preparation for this celebration of workers is a chance for classes to connect with people in different careers. All subject areas should be represented with in-person and online opportunities to meet workers and question them about their career preparation and job responsibilities. Connect with classes in other countries to determine when and how this holiday is celebrated where they live. Connecting with other classrooms in the United States might be more of a challenge for this holiday in light of the fact that not everyone starts school before **Labor Day**. Find out why other schools always start after Labor Day.

September 11: Showing Compassion

Find out how different communities in the United States and in other countries commemorate the attack on the United States that took place on **September 11, 2001**. This also presents a chance for students to connect with people who experienced this event personally or those willing to share their reaction to what happened on that day. Try to connect with people and get their feelings about the events that occurred in New York City, Washington, DC, and western Pennsylvania. Jerry, in a Skype call, was interviewed by a class about where he was and how he felt upon learning what happened on September 11. The call also covered Jerry's reactions to President Kennedy's assassination on November 22, 1963, and to the space shuttle *Challenger* disaster on January 28, 1986.

Hispanic Heritage Month (September 15–October 15)

Each year in the United States, National **Hispanic Heritage Month** is observed from September 15 to October 15. There are many ways to celebrate the histories, cultures, and contributions of American citizens whose ancestors came from Spain, Mexico, the Caribbean, and Central and South America. The Latin American countries of Costa Rica, El Salvador, Guatemala, Honduras, and Nicaragua observe their independence anniversary on September 15. Mexico celebrates its independence on September 16, while Chile celebrates its independence on September 18.

   Columbus Day also falls within this 30-day period. This is a good opportunity to connect a class in a Spanish-speaking country with a class in a non-Spanish-speaking country. Have students come up with questions about their school day, culture, customs, holidays, history, and traditions. Carrying out these conversations can lead to collaborations in all subject areas.

International Dot Day* (September 15)

How will you make your mark on September 15? **International Dot Day** is based on Peter H. Reynolds's book *The Dot*.[1] Terry Shay, a teacher in Iowa, decided to start this project after reading Reynolds's book to his class in 2009. Just like the main character in the book, students are encouraged to make their mark and share it with the world.

Terry has created a website, International Dot Day, where you can register and find a wealth of ideas and materials to help you and your students be part of this international project.[2]

When author Sharon Creech (*Love That Dog, Walk Two Moons*) sent Terry her dot in 2011, he started the Celebri-dot site.[3] This is where he posts dots created by authors, sports figures, actors, and other celebrities who want to leave their mark.

Paula Naugle invited Rachel Schmidt's pre-K class to join her fourth graders for the festivities during the closing event of one of her Dot Day collaboration. The older students led the little ones through a series of stations they had set up in their classroom. Using bingo stampers, Paula's students helped their little buddies write their name with dots. They used a collection of dot-shaped objects to help the pre-K kids create collage-type pictures. Then all the students took turns playing Twister.

Paula's class also Skyped with author Laurie Ann Thompson (@LaurieThompson), and they played Mystery Skype with her to learn that she is located in Washington. They also did a Skype call with the famous storyteller Mrs. P (@MrsPstoryTime, Kathy Kinney) from California. Mrs. P shared her Celebri-dot[4] with the students and they shared their creations with her. The two classes ended their Dot Day celebration by eating donut holes and Dots candies.

A couple of years ago, Paula, who teaches in Louisiana, had a different kind of Dot Day collaboration. She was invited to Skype into Marialice BFX Curran's (@mbfxc) class of pre-service teachers in Connecticut to explain how she collaborates with other classrooms. Paula shared her students' dot creations and told how her class had shared their dots during the day with their Skype buddy class in Kansas.

Classrooms from around the world have connected and collaborated with others via video conferencing, building **wikis** and web pages, and sharing blog posts and videos to celebrate how they left their mark on International Dot Day.

Dot Day has been around for a long time as you can tell from these stories and there are so many different ways to celebrate it. International Dot Day is still celebrated across schools today. Make sure you also follow #InternationalDotDay as well as check out www.thedotclub.org/dotday/.

October Projects

LGBT History Month

Schools should ensure that there are safe spaces for students who identify as LGBTQ. Such as a club or a group where students can get together and feel safe. Schools and districts should make sure that classroom libraries feature non stereotypical LGBTQ characters from kindergarten and up. Bring in a guest speaker to discuss LGBT issues that students might face or ways to believe in yourself.

> Open to ALL: Serving the GLBT Community in Your Library—American Library Association www.ala.org/rt/sites/ala.org.rt/files/content/professionaltools/160309-glbtrt-open-to-all-toolkit-online.pdf
> LGBTQIA+ Resources for Children: A Bibliography | Round Tables—American Library Association www.ala.org/rt/rrt/popularresources/children
> Stonewall Book Awards List www.ala.org/rt/rrt/award/stonewall/honored
> Check out Jerry's LGBTQ Students page: www.cybraryman.com/lgbt.html

Indigenous Peoples' Day

"Indigenous Peoples' Day recognizes that Native people are the first inhabitants of the Americas, including the lands that later became the United States of America. And it urges Americans to rethink history."[5] As we talk about projects for Native American Heritage Month you can have students do research to find out the Native American tribes that lived in their towns or cities.

Take a virtual trip to the National Museum of Native American Indian: https://americanindian.si.edu/online-resources/exhibition-websites
Resources for teaching and learning:

> www.smithsonianmag.com/blogs/national-museum-american-indian/2019/10/11/indigenous-peoples-day-2019/
> www.cnn.com/2019/04/22/us/indigenous-peoples-day-columbus-day-trnd/index.html
> Inclusive Booklists | American Library Association www.ala.org/aboutala/offices/diversity/literacy/inclusive-booklist

How Weather Affects Us*

The fall season is a chance for classes experiencing the changing of leaf colors to compare notes with other students around the country and the world who do not experience this seasonal change. The science behind the changing of leaf colors (**photosynthesis**) can be explored. Classes in different parts of the world can share the difference in climate and compare temperatures.

Paula (in Louisiana), Billy (in New Jersey), and Nancy Carroll, a fourth-grade teacher in Massachusetts, spent several Sunday evenings putting together a collaborative project for their classes by doing a Google Hangout with each other. The project they created was called "How Weather Affects Us."

Paula's students created surveys about weather using Google Forms. By tweeting out the **URL**s to their surveys, they were able to collect weather data from many states in the United States and from countries including Great Britain, New Zealand, and the United Arab Emirates. The three classes then held Skype calls to discuss the data and decided to create poster graphs in their math classes. Billy's students did a Google Hangout to show Paula's students how to enter the data into Excel spreadsheets to create online graphs. To make this project even more collaborative, you can now use Google Sheets or Excel in Office 365 to work together in real time to update the weather in different parts of the country or the world.

Halloween Projects

Halloween provides the opportunity to have your students be very creative. Have them write a trick-or-treat or scary story, put on a play, or make a movie. You can also do a multimedia project that gives younger children important safety information for when they go trick or treating. Share your projects and work with another class via Google Docs to connect and create a joint activity.

November Projects

Election Day

The issues raised in political campaigns provide an opportunity to have an online debate between classes in different localities. A Google Meet can be used not only to have the classes shown but to allow for judges to view the proceedings. **Virtual debates** occur when classes in different locations carry out a debate on a topic via Skype or Google Meet. A virtual debate is another easy way to connect classrooms as students can research and debate a topic of either the teacher's choosing or a topic that students are interested in researching.

Connect with a class in another school and do a mock campaign for office. Have students give two-minute speeches. If possible, do this for class elections. Have each opposing class vote for who they would want for class officers in the other class based on their speeches. It would be interesting to see who the other class would elect for positions not really knowing the candidates, which could help remove the popularity aspect of class elections.

Veterans Day/Remembrance Day

To honor those who have served while allowing children to gain knowledge of the wars and conflicts our countries have been involved in, this holiday allows for connections with veterans. Local veterans' organizations can bring together students and veterans willing to be interviewed by students. These interviews can be conducted via a Skype call, Google Meet, or a Zoom call.

Connect with classes in Canada, England, or Australia to learn how they celebrate **Remembrance Day** and then compare it to the way Veterans Day is celebrated in the United States.

Gettysburg Address*

In honor of the 150th anniversary of the Gettysburg Address, Billy did a Google Hangout (with schools in California and Tennessee. Students from each class read a section of the address for the others on a Google Hangout. The students were interested in celebrating this milestone event and were excited to connect with other classes. Students not only recited the Gettysburg Address but also asked each other questions about the significance of this historical document. Consider connecting with a classroom on November 19 (President Lincoln on November 19, 1863 gave this speech at the dedication of the Soldiers' National Cemetery in Gettysburg, Pennsylvania) to read and discuss the Gettysburg Address. You can even take a virtual tour of the battlefield of Gettysburg. We discuss virtual field trips in Chapter 6 but here is the link for the virtual tour of Gettysburg: www.battlefields.org/visit/virtual-tours/gettysburg-360-virtual-tour.

Native American Heritage Month

When Jerry went to elementary school, each year some Hopi Indians came to his school and talked about their customs and culture. It was quite fascinating to learn about them. Jerry made it a point to teach his students about the Native American tribe that inhabited the land in what is now their school neighborhood. Have your students do research to find out the Native American tribes that lived in their towns or cities. Then take the next step by reaching out to connect with members of that tribe. You can also do a Mystery Tribe Call with another class and have them try to determine the Native American tribe you are describing. See if you can find a story about Native Americans who inhabited your area of the country and share the story with another classroom via video.

Thanksgiving Day: Canada (October) vs. the United States (November)

Connect classes in Canada with those in the United States to discuss why and how Thanksgiving is celebrated in these two countries at different times in the fall. Many countries celebrate harvest festivals. Have your students discover how other countries celebrate harvests and then try to connect with classes in those countries to compare and contrast. When discussing Thanksgiving it is important to discuss all the aspects of Thanksgiving, and as educators we should also consider discussing the view point of Thanksgiving from the Native American standpoint. As Native Americans do not celebrate Thanksgiving, they partake in the National Day of Mourning, which takes place on the fourth Thursday of November.

> *If this date sounds familiar to you, it's because the fourth Thursday of November also coincides with Thanksgiving in the U.S. Every year on the National Day of Mourning, Native American people in New England gather together to protest. To them, Thanksgiving serves as a reminder of the unjust treatment that Native Americans have received since the 1620 Plymouth landing.[6]*

Plimoth Plantation*

What better way to learn about **Plimoth Plantation** than to take a virtual field trip there (we go into depth about virtual field trips in Chapter 6)? Billy was able to connect with Nancy Carroll to bring his students along with Nancy's students as they visited Plimoth Plantation. Nancy explained how she was able to share her field trip virtually:

> *Using my smartphone and Skype, the class wandered in and out of the Plimoth Village (in real-time) and had several opportunities to listen to the Pilgrims as they spoke with my students. Questions from the New Jersey students were relayed to the Pilgrims via my students (as folks in the 1620's would never have understood a smartphone never mind Skype!).*

December Projects

Pearl Harbor Day

December 7, 1941, is a fateful day in American history, the day Japan attacked the naval base at Pearl Harbor in Hawaii. Have students do some research on the events of this day and try to connect with older adults who remember this event and get their reaction to what transpired as a result of this attack. The same can be done for other important dates in history, such as President Kennedy's assassination, the *Challenger* explosion, and September 11. Students can be connected to other students in programs such as Edmodo, **Google Classroom**, and VoiceThread to discuss these events and take different viewpoints. Take the students on a virtual tour of Pearl Harbor (https:// ussmissouri.org/press/press-releases/take-a-free-virtual-field-trip-of-the-battleship-missouri-memorial-online-classroom-experience-for-students-grades-5-through-12).

Sharing Different Holiday Celebrations

When I taught, I would put the important events of the day on the board. I also had a posted calendar of the month on oak tag which showed the different holidays and celebrations all over the world. I wanted my students to know about these events and their significance and how different cultures celebrated holidays. Whenever school was closed, I wanted the students to know what the holiday was all about and not just that there was no school on that day. They learned about the biggest holidays around the world: Christmas, Hanukkah, New Year's, Chinese or Lunar New Year, Ramadan and Eid al-Fitr, Easter, Valentine's Day, Diwali and Bodhi Day.

Holidays make for a great way to connect with students all over the world and find out the similarities and differences on how they are celebrated. One of my classes wanted to find out what foods people around the world ate during the December holidays. They connected with students all over the world and found out some very interesting traditions. They corresponded with students from other countries got their recipes and with the help of parents celebrated a multicultural December Holidays feast.

January Projects

New Year's

The New Year provides a wonderful opportunity to connect your class with another in a foreign country to find out how they celebrate this day. Include in your discussions with these students making resolutions and how to keep them.

Dr. Martin Luther King, Jr.*

There are many different ways you can connect with other classrooms about Dr. Martin Luther King, Jr. One way is to organize an online short speech competition with another class with the theme of civil rights using nonviolent civil disobedience as practiced by Dr. King. Using a Google Meet, you can have a panel of judges from other locations decide which class won. Connect through various websites such as Edmodo, Google Classroom, or VoiceThread; allow students to share essays based on the theme "I Have a Dream" or let them collaborate on a speech they would give.

Martin's Big Words*

Billy worked with Connie Fink on a collaborative project about the civil rights movement. This project involved a third-grade class and a sixth-grade class; the students discussed the civil rights movement using the book *Martin's Big Words*. The questions and quotes that were discussed follow:

- Why do you think these "white only" signs were present in Southern cities and towns in the United States?
- Who was Mahatma Gandhi and how did he influence the civil rights movement in the United States?
- *Martin's Big Words*: "Hate cannot drive out hate. Only love can do that."
- How would people react today if they were sitting next to Rosa Parks and she was asked to "get up from her seat"? What makes today's reaction different from 1955?
- Why was the strategy *not* to ride "buses until they could sit anywhere they wanted" a good one (boycotting)? Did it follow Gandhi's way of thinking?
- Wow, 381 days! Would you be able/willing to walk to school in the "rain and cold and in blistering heat"? In what ways did Dr. Martin Luther King, Jr. walking and talking with them, singing and praying, give the African Americans strength?
- *Martin's Big Words*: "Wait! For years I have heard the word 'Wait!' We have waited more than 340 years."
- *Martin's Big Words*: "Love is the key to the problems of the world."
- *Martin's Big Words*: "Remember, if I am stopped, this movement will not be stopped, because God is with this movement."
- "He won it because he taught others to fight with words not fists." What can we learn in our own lives from this thought?
- "His big words are alive for us today." What can we do to continue to keep his words alive today?

100th Day of School*

The commemoration of the **100th day of school** occurs at different times depending upon the first day of school where you live. There are many creative ways to celebrate this event. Connect with other classes to find out what they will be doing on this day. Share different ways to celebrate the 100th day of school in all subject areas. Find a class on Skype or Google Meet and have a joint celebration. Students can discuss how they counted to 100 days of school or they can share 100 facts about their town, city, or state. Have older students write a 100-word poem or song about school.

February Projects

American Heart Month*

The prevention of heart disease should start with our adolescents. There is an epidemic of obesity and other unhealthy habits among our youth. We need to get young people thinking about ways to be healthy. Jerry enjoys passing an elementary school and watching students jogging around the campus. He likes seeing a middle school that has a Mile Club and remembering his own children having to do a mile run. Find out what other schools are doing about keeping fit. Set up discussions of healthy habits and then start competitions between two classes in different locations via Skype or Google Meet. Have students set up a spreadsheet to keep track of the distance they walk or run each day. Show them apps they can use on their mobile devices to track their fitness. Involve parents and work with them on ways to keep their children fit.

Physical education departments in many schools have students compete in Jump Rope for Heart during this time of the year as well. At Paula's school the students post graphs in the main lobby to show how much money each grade level has collected. Younger students love graphing how many jumps they do each day for the week. Older students keep track of their heart rate before and after jumping rope. To make Jump Rope for Heart a collaborative project, send out a tweet or Facebook post asking for a partner school with which to compare results. Connect the classrooms via Skype or Google Meet and let the students share their results, demonstrate their best jump-roping skills, or sing their favorite jump-rope songs.

Black History Month*

February is celebrated as Black History Month. Engage another class in a competition to determine if they can figure out the famous black person you are describing. This activity will be similar to the Olympics challenge we did with several classes. It was a fun challenge where clever questions were raised and so much was learned. Share information about famous black people in your town, city, state, and country with other classes around the country or the world. Have your students prepare reports about a famous living black person. This will enhance their research skills and their ability to find accurate information from reliable sources.

The #K12Valentine Project

Here is a project from our PLN member Nancy Carroll:

The idea behind this project is to connect virtually and make someone smile! Students created virtual valentines (one class used Book Creator and another class used Google Drawings, although there are a great many programs that can be used).

Teachers posted the finished valentines on Twitter using the hashtag #k12Valentine. After posting, the teachers and students scrolled through the posts with the hashtag and read the valentines from around the globe! They had fun reading and viewing the movies made by others. (Next year, one teacher assured me she was going to connect with another class—an optional component—during this project.)

This meaningful project was quick and easy to get started. It can lead to general connections or specific connections. It was inspiring to see so many creative valentines which surely lifted the spirits of many!

Lunar New Year

Students can first find out from other classes in Chinatowns across this country how they celebrate the Lunar New Year. Then they can connect with students in other countries like Cambodia, Vietnam, China, Korea, and the Philippines to learn how they celebrate the Lunar New Year. One idea would be to connect with educators from cities such as New York and San Francisco that have Chinatowns.

Groundhog Day

The yearly Groundhog Day event on February 2 is an opportunity to learn about the seasons, climate, light, shadows, and solar observations. Have the classes do some research on the location of Punxsutawney, Pennsylvania, and the accuracy of their "early spring" statistics throughout the years. Reach out to classes in other locations to compare daily weather and climate. Have students keep daily charts of sunrise, sunset, temperature, and other weather facts. Each class should then offer their own predictions and periodically connect with the other class to see how their predictions have turned out. These connections can be used through a variety of formats; Edmodo, Google Classroom, Google Docs, and VoiceThread are just a few tools with which students can use to collaborate.

Super Bowl Connections*

When the New York Giants and New England Patriots both reached the Super Bowl for the first time, Billy (from New Jersey, a fan of the New York Giants) and Nancy (from Massachusetts, a fan of the New England Patriots) had their very first Mystery Skype Call the Monday after both teams made it into the Super Bowl. As the Mystery Skype Call went on and the two classes discovered each other's location, they realized that Billy's school was within a ten-minute drive of Giants Stadium and that Nancy's school was almost across the street from Gillette Stadium. At that point, Nancy and Billy decided to connect their classes beyond the Mystery Skype Call and that the classes would do something related to the Super Bowl.

After much discussion, the two decided to learn all about the state in which the Super Bowl was taking place. That year it was Indianapolis, Indiana. Nancy and Billy had their classes explore different facts about the state. The students learned about the geography, demographics, natural features, resources, products, and borders of Indiana. They also learned more about the city of Indianapolis. The two classes met again on the Friday before the Super Bowl and shared what they had learned. The students in both classes wore their home teams' jerseys. It was a great way to have the students connect beyond the Mystery Skype Call, and of course the classes did have a little wager going on. As a result, Nancy had a Giants pennant hanging in her classroom for the rest of the school year.

Sports are great ways to use mathematics in education because math is applied constantly in all sporting events. Math provides opportunities to study player and team statistics, distances, probability, and percentages. You can have students determine how many more yards a player needs to run to get a first down, or the percentage of caught passes thrown by the quarterback, or how much time has elapsed in the game. Mathematics is in all sports, so this is a great way to engage those students who might have a huge interest in sports but don't see the connection between sports and what they are learning in school. Children can try to guess the final score of a football game using different variations of touchdowns, field goals, safeties, extra points, and even missed extra points. Have students find the statistics on their favorite players on the major sports leagues pages and compare them to other similar players.

Here is a story about the National Football League playoff to decide who would go to the Super Bowl from one of our PLN members, Jennifer Regruth. She made a connection through Nancy Carroll, another #4thchat participant. Nancy's former principal teaches at a school right across from the Patriots' stadium. He was initiating a program to connect with other schools near the stadium where the Patriots were playing to promote good sportsmanship. Jennifer set up the connection with a fourth-grade classroom in Massachusetts and planned a time to have a Google Hangout. The teachers collaborated and decided to use math to guess the score, and each side came up with different ways to get that score. For example, if Jennifer's school in Indiana picked the score of 24–21 for a Colts win, did they get the points through touchdowns, extra points, field goals, or safeties? The students had fun guessing. Each school was wearing the gear of their favorite team and showing handmade signs to support their team. The students and teachers wished each other luck. The two classes actually connected twice because they did a video chat during the regular season and then again in the playoffs. As demonstrated by Jennifer's story, you can also apply mathematics to an event like the National Football League playoffs and make the event more educationally meaningful to the students.

Another great project to do during the Super Bowl is the "Souper Bowl of Caring," an event that takes place around the same time as the Super Bowl, where students collect cans of soup to donate to local food pantries. You can connect with other classrooms participating in this national program and have a friendly competition. You can graph the number of cans your students collect daily, break down the different types of soups that you have collected, and take a survey of students' favorite soups. All of these activities can be done both in your school and with other classrooms across the United States. For more information about the "Souper Bowl of Caring," visit www.souper bowl.org/.

Presidents' Day

Connect with another class and discuss the characteristics of a good leader. Compare types of government with classes around the world. Find out the different forms of government in your town and city and what leaders are needed. Invite a local leader into your classroom in person or via Skype or Google Meet. Have your students do some research and then plan appropriate questions beforehand. Carry out an interview with the leader. Divide your students into different groups to work with other classrooms from around the country in Google Classroom or Edmodo. Post questions to one another and have them research the questions. Create a multimedia project on the US presidents using their quotations and sound clips of them. You can also put together some fun facts and historical details. Have students conduct mock interviews of a famous president. Have students research the pros and cons that presidents have on all communities. Students can conduct research about the different political parties and what the parties represent. Remember that communities are affected differently by the president that is elected and educators should allow students to have an understanding of how these differences can affect a community.

The Winter Olympics

The Olympic Games garner a lot of attention every two years, alternating between Summer and Winter Games. Students are excited about the Olympics Games, therefore it becomes an engaging way to get students excited about learning. The Olympic Games allow us to be able to teach many different subject areas at once. We can discuss geography, mathematics, and science all in one lesson while getting students excited about the subject. This is also relevant to what is going on in the world around us. Today, we are even able to connect with each other about the Olympics and with athletes in the Olympic Village.

Several members of #4thchat were lucky enough to be able to connect during the 2014 Winter Olympics and had a friendly little competition with our classrooms doing an Olympic Game Show. Another great way of exposing students to the sporting and cultural events is to video conference with the Olympic Village. Jennifer Regruth was able to connect her classroom and shared her experience with the historic event and even how she obtained this exciting opportunity in Chapter 2.

Notes

1. www.peterhreynolds.com/dot/.
2. www.thedotclub.org/dotday/.
3. www.celebridots.com.
4. www.celebridots.com/2013/09/mrs-p-kathy-kinney.html.
5. www.smithsonianmag.com/blogs/national-museum-american-indian/2019/10/11/indigenous-peoples-day-2019/.
6. https://nationaltoday.com/national-day-of-mourning/.

Resources

Black History: www.cybraryman.com/blackhistory.html
Celebri-dots: www.celebridots.com
Chinese New Year: www.cybraryman.com/chinesenewyear.html
Civil Rights Movement: www.cybraryman.com/civilrights.html
Civil War (Gettysburg): www.cybraryman.com/civilwar.html
Debate: www.cybraryman.com/debate.html

Dot Day: www.cybraryman.com/dotday.html
Dr. Martin Luther King, Jr.: www.cybraryman.com/mlk.html
Election Day: www.cybraryman.com/elections.html
Fall: www.cybraryman.com/fall.html
Groundhog Day: www.cybraryman.com/groundhog.html
Halloween: www.cybraryman.com/halloween.html
Harvest Festivals From Around the World: www.harvestfestivals.net/har
    vestfestivals.htm
Hispanic Heritage: www.cybraryman.com/hispanic.html
International Dot Day: https://cybraryman.com/dotday.html; www.thedot
    club.org/dotday
Labor History: www.cybraryman.com/laborhistory.html
Laurie Ann Thompson: www.twitter.com/lauriethompson
Mrs. P's Magic Library: www.mrsp.com
Native Americans: www.cybraryman.com/nativeamericans.html
New Year's: www.cybraryman.com/new_years.html
Plimoth Plantation: www.plimoth.org
Presidents' Day: www.cybraryman.com/presidents.html
Resolutions: www.cybraryman.com/resolutions2.html
September 11: www.cybraryman.com/september11.html
Super Bowl/Football: www.cybraryman.com/football.html
Thanksgiving: www.cybraryman.com/thanksgiving.html
Valentine's Day: www.cybraryman.com/valentine.html
Veterans Day/Remembrance Day: www.cybraryman.com/veteransday.html
Winter/Snow Fun: www.cybraryman.com/snow.html
100th Day of School: www.cybraryman.com/100thday1.html

The Next Chapter

In Chapter 5, we will explore ways to celebrate holidays and events that occur during the spring and summer seasons and possibilities for connecting your students with other classes. It will provide teachers with ideas for celebrations with their students and others across the country and the world.

5

Spring and Summer Projects

When reviewing and reading these projects, remember that we are just giving you ideas and ways to possibly connect your classroom. These projects can all be adapted to meet the technology available for your class, school, and district.

In this chapter, we are going to explore different projects that could be implemented during the spring and summer, ones we have either participated in or heard about. These projects usually occur during March, April, May, June, July, and August. We have also included ideas about how to celebrate holidays and events that occur during this season.

This is meant to be a practical guide for finding projects that are useful and ways in which to start collaborating. These projects can be used as a follow-up to Mystery Location Calls or as separate projects to connect your students with other classrooms. The asterisk (*) indicates projects that we have participated in. If there is not an asterisk (*), these are ideas or suggestions that you could expand upon in your classroom.

March Projects

Mardi Gras*

Mardi Gras is a unique celebration, and many students do not know the true meaning behind it. Paula teaches in New Orleans and has had her students do research on different aspects of Mardi Gras. During the two weeks leading up

Spring and Summer Projects

March
Mardi Gras*
Read Across America—Dr. Seuss's Birthday*
Commonwealth Day
Pi Day—March 14 (3/14)
St. Patrick's Day*
Women's History Month

April
National Autism Awareness Month
Impromptu Calls*
Poetry Month*
Baseball
Holocaust Remembrance Day
Earth Day—Groceries Project*
Arbor Day

May
National Inventors Month
10-Day Passion Challenge and Identity Day*
Cinco de Mayo (5th of May)*
Memorial Day

June
Flag Day
Graduation—End of School

Billy Krakower
@wkrakower

@plnaugle My students loved your students Mardi Gras presentation. Thanks for including us.

8:01 PM - 10 Feb 2012

Figure 5.1 Tweet That Billy Sent Out After the Mardi Gras Event

to this celebration, Paula's students share their firsthand experience with other classes. Paula invites other classrooms to learn about Mardi Gras through Skype or Google Meet. She sends out a Google Form for classes to sign up so they can come into her class and learn. This is a great example of ways to share the learning experience from your classroom with other classrooms.

Linda Yollis wrote a blog post about the time she participated in the Mardi Gras Skype call.[1] Patti Grayson also posted about the Mardi Gras Skype call.[2] See Figure 5.1 as Billy Tweeted to Paula's class thanking them for including his class.

Read Across America—Dr. Seuss's Birthday
As part of **Read Across America**, Jerry had the distinct pleasure to read *The Cat in the Hat Comes Back* to classes in Indiana, Louisiana, Massachusetts, Michigan, New Jersey, and Pennsylvania as part of a Google Meet.

This special event was also seen by classes all over the world on YouTube. Jerry shared many interesting facts about Dr. Seuss because he spent a lot of time in Seuss's hometown of Springfield, Massachusetts, where Jerry's wife also grew up. This was a great way for the students involved to expand their connections from Mystery Location Calls, as most of the classes had previously participated in such calls together (Blumengarten, 2013).

Commonwealth Day

Commonwealth Day is a celebration of the Commonwealth of Nations that is held on the second Monday in March. It is also a chance to understand the cooperative work on Commonwealth organizations. Have your students do research on what countries constituted the Commonwealth of Nations and how they work together. Connect with classes that celebrate this annual event to find out more about it.

Pi Day—March 14 (3/14)

Pi Day (celebrated on March 14, to represent the value of π, 3.14) is a great way to do some cross-curricular work focusing especially on mathematics. Have your students come up with Pi Day activities that will appeal to all of their senses. Students can create learning board or computer games that involve the use of π. Connect with other classes to brainstorm ways to celebrate Pi Day with activities and projects in all subject areas. Read *Sir Cumference and the Dragon of Pi*, which is a great story to get the conversation started about what π is. There are a number of amazing stories in the Sir Cumference series as well.[3] Conduct surveys through various social media channels and have students create pi graphs. Students can share and analyze data during a Google Meet or Skype call.

St. Patrick's Day*

Ireland is rich in castles and their history. Students can learn about the history of Ireland and its legends, as well as facts and fiction about St. Patrick's Day. Bring students to Ireland by visiting Castles of Northern Ireland on Virtual Visit Tours and taking virtual tours of the castles in Ireland.[4] Students can connect with other classrooms or write a blog post if they celebrate St. Patrick's Day and discuss family traditions around the holiday.

Women's History Month

In a spin-off of the Mystery Location Call in honor of Women's History Month, have your students come up with five-minute oral presentations on famous women. The students can dress up as the woman they chose to study if they wish. They should also respond to questions as if they were in that time period. Each class will take turns presenting, and the other class has to figure out who the mystery woman is. Each oral presentation should last around five minutes. Listening skills will be essential to help pick up on clues in each presentation. Researchers must be able to find accurate information quickly. Students should prepare for these Mystery Woman Calls by practicing their search skills along with their ability to evaluate information. Make sure to assign jobs for all the students in the class during the call. You will need researchers, questioners, and fact-checkers, as well as the normal Mystery Location Call jobs. Additionally, ensure that students report on why they chose this person to study.

April Projects

National Autism Awareness Month

Have your students do research on autism. Arrange a connection with another class to allow your students share their knowledge about autism and help spread awareness and acceptance of those with autism and anyone who is different. Try to have an autism expert come into your class in person or virtually. Start an autism awareness campaign in your school led by your students. After reading such books as *Since We're Friends: An Autism Picture Book*, *I'm Here*, or *Different Like Me: My Book of Autism Heroes*, discuss what was learned and how everyone can be more understanding of students with developmental disabilities.

Impromptu Calls*

During one #4thchat on Twitter a couple of years ago, Paula started a discussion about doing impromptu Skype calls when standardized testing was over. She started a Google Doc and asked other interested teachers to sign up. They indicated which days they would be available to take an impromptu call. By keeping Skype open on their computer, they would know when a call was coming in. If they could take a video call, they would answer, and the two classes would chat with each other and bring each other up to date on what was happening in their classroom and in their community. These were great calls to make between classes that had connected during the year. The students shared their writings, their artwork, and their favorite movies, books, and games. One time a class even shared what made each person unique.

On one such impromptu Skype call, Paula's class placed a call to Jan Wells, the teacher of their Skype buddy class in Kansas, and was surprised when Jan answered because she had a classroom full of teachers instead of her students. She was conducting an in-service about using Skype to connect with other classes. What perfect timing! The students shared with these teachers the Earth Day grocery bags they had just finished decorating.

Doing impromptu Skype calls or impromptu Google Meets is a very relaxed way to keep your connections going. There is no advanced planning involved. You simply place the call and have a conversation. Think of all of the topics of conversation that you could initiate between two or more classes. They also are a great way to let students direct their own learning as they decide what topic of conversation they would like.

Poetry Month*

Have your students either write their own poem or copy a favorite poem and put it in their pocket. This activity is part of Poetry Month's Poem in Your Pocket Day at the end of April. Poetry Month gives students the opportunity to create different types of poems, such as acrostic, blank verse, cinquain, free verse, haiku, limerick, lyric, narrative, rhyme, shape, tanka, and visual. Employ technology to produce the poems. Have a poetry slam (where students read their original poems) on a Google Meet with several classes and use another class to judge them.

Here is a story about a poetry summit from Elissa Malespina (@elissamalespina), a member of our PLN from New Jersey.

The idea for a Poetry Summit started with ways to connect kids virtually and show their love of poetry. Frances Ann Squire from Birchwood Intermediate School on Prince Edward Island, Canada, Shawn Storm from Strayer Middle School in Quakertown, PA, Elissa Malespina and Melissa Butler from South Orange Middle School in South Orange, New Jersey and Janelle Thompson and Shannon McClintock Miller from Van Meter Community School in Van Meter, Iowa, all came together to have students connect via Edmodo, and Google Meet. During the Poetry Summit students not only read the poetry they created, but also got to hear poems from famous poets like Robert Forbes, and Tina Kelly. Ms. P from Ms. Ps storytime also made a guest appearance. During the second year of the summit, we expanded it from a 2 hour event to a full day event. We even added a kickoff event where we had a college professor come in and teach the students a lesson on creating poetry. Using Google Meet, we recorded the event so that any school who was participating could use the lesson with their students even if they could not be there for the lesson in person. Many more schools participated in last years' summit including some from Hawaii and Canada. The event also became international with the addition of the Shakespeare HipHop company who joined us from London, England. None of this would have been possible without technology like Google Meet! Students still talk about the event to this day!

Baseball

The start of the baseball season lends itself to many different ways to celebrate this sport. Math plays a big part in baseball, and you can have students find and keep track of their favorite players and team statistics.

For social studies activities you can map the location and distances between cities of rival teams and find the derivation of your team's name. Connect with students in other areas of the country or Canada to play math or trivia baseball games of your making. Have students conduct research on the history of baseball and connect with students in states that are home to the original baseball teams. You can book a video conference call with the National Baseball Hall of Fame.[5]

Use your math skills and do virtual visits of other baseball stadiums and then compare the difference in distance of the stadiums, the seating capacity, and other stadium statistics.

Holocaust Remembrance Day

If possible, host a Skype call or a Google Meet with a Holocaust survivor or have them come to your school to have them tell their story and even, with their permission, record the session to save as an oral history. Prepare your students with lessons on the Holocaust and have them think of pertinent questions for the interview. If you are unable to contact an actual Holocaust survivor, connect with the staff at the Holocaust Survivors and Victims Resource Center at the United States Holocaust Memorial Museum to ask them questions your students have researched.

Visit Yad Vashem's Holocaust History Museum virtually.[6] Yad Vashem is located in Israel and is the World Center for Holocaust Research, Education, Documentation, and Commemoration. This is another easy way in which to have your students learn about a historic event. Students can then write blog posts about what they have learned from their experience. Upper elementary and middle school students can read *Anne Frank: Diary of a Young Girl*, *The Boy in the Striped Pyjamas* by John Boyne, *Number the Stars* by Lois Lowry, *The Book Thief* by Markus Zusak, or *Night* by Elie Wiesel. *The Boy in the Striped Pyjamas* is also a movie, which can be viewed after the book is read. Then students can discuss these books and movies using Google Classroom, Edmodo, VoiceThread, and other forms of social media for connecting students.

Earth Day—Groceries Project*

Earth Day, April 22, is the opportunity to focus on our environment and how to improve it. Have your students come up with some ways to prevent waste or clean up the school or community. Simple things like recycling materials can go a long way toward preserving the environment. A great place to bring items for recycling and turn them into useful items is through a **Makerspace**, which are popping up in libraries and schools around the world. Work with the school administrators, custodial staff, and other staff members on ways to be more environmentally responsible within the school community. Also include the parents of your students in discussions of environmental issues.

One Earth Day project Paula has done allows her students to collaborate within their own community. The Earth Day Groceries Project has you get brown paper bags from your local grocery store and decorate them with Earth Day art and messages.[7]

At the beginning of April, Paula contacts a local grocery store and arranges to pick up a bundle of their brown paper bags. The students do math calculations to figure out how many bags they need to decorate a day in order to have all 400 bags completed before Earth Day. Her students than decorate the bags with Earth-friendly messages and artwork. The bags are returned to the store a few days before April 22, which is Earth Day. The students love seeing their bags going out into their greater community. We have turned this collaboration into another math lesson by figuring out how many trees are used to produce the brown bags for the grocery store each year. We also compare and contrast paper bags to plastic bags, and this year we will be adding reusable grocery bags to the mix. Check out Paula's YouTube video about her Earth Day Groceries Project (www.youtube.com/watch?v=fv0JRv5ZPQI).

Another idea is for students to do short research projects about environmental heroes. Paula created an Environmental Heroes **WebQuest** that can help get you started.[8] The next step to make this a collaborative project is to find other classes to video conference with and share your research projects.

Arbor Day

Arbor Day, observed on the last Friday in April, is a holiday to get people to plant or care for trees. Share with another class that you connect with about your state tree and the different types of trees in your area. Discuss the similarities and differences of the trees in each class's region. Determine what effects the location or climate has on the type of trees in their locations. Set up a competition with another class, which could include showing pictures and playing "Name that Tree." Have students do research to come up with three trivia questions.

May Projects

National Inventors Month

With makerspaces being so popular in today's educational world, what better way to celebrate National Inventors Month than to talk with inventors and then let students become their own inventors? Makerspaces are an area where students get to become the inventor. Take students on a virtual field trip to the Smithsonian Institute. Have your students share their creations with other classes or have a Makerspace competition.

A great article to read with students is "May Is National Inventors Month."[9] Students can research different inventors and share the inventions they create themselves.

10-Day Passion Challenge and Identity Day*

Have you heard of Identity Day, #GeniusHour, 20%time, or Passion Learning? Many teachers have found a way to incorporate the time in their weekly schedule to allow students to pursue their passions. Usually an hour a week is set aside when the students can spend time directing their own learning about a topic they are passionate about.

Several of our PLN members wanted to do something like this with their students but could not find the time within their regular teaching schedule to do so. Paula decided that during May (her last month of school each year), there would be time available for her students to pursue a passion project for a two-week period. She put together a 10-Day Passion Challenge on a Google Doc and invited other interested teachers to join in with their students. Each participating class joined an Edmodo group, and each day a question was posted that got students thinking about their passion. Within the Edmodo group they could respond to the daily question and to other students' responses by using the @ in front of the student's name (for example, @Eric S.). You can also create a Google Classroom to complete these projects.

At the end of the two weeks, interested classes set a date to connect with each other and hold an Identity Day. During Identity Day the classes connected via Skype or Google Meet and shared their passion projects, which came in a variety of formats, such as traditional trifold presentation boards, **Glogsters**, videos, blog posts, and more.

Cinco de Mayo (5th of May)*

This holiday is an opportunity to learn about other cultures. Have your students find out more about the history of Cinco de Mayo. Encourage them to create projects to illustrate **cultural responsiveness**. Students can connect with other classes and share their illustrations or try and connect with classes in Mexico and interview students to find out the origins of Cinco de Mayo.

Paula's students were treated to a wonderful performance by Louise Morgan's second graders for Cinco de Mayo. Mrs. Morgan, who teaches in San Antonio, Texas, broadcasted her students' presentation via her **Ustream** channel.

Memorial Day

Celebrated on the last Monday in May, Memorial Day presents the opportunity to interview those who have served in the military to find out the importance of this holiday. Connect with other classes around the world to see what they do to honor those who served and died in battle. Work with veterans' groups to help plant flags in military cemeteries to commemorate those who have fallen.

June Projects

Flag Day

Have a flag recognition competition call with another class in honor of Flag Day (June 14). Show the flag of each country around the world and give some hints as to its location. The class that comes up with the most correct country flags will be declared the winner. Share with the other class the countries of the world that the students and staff of the school represent. Work together with your students to develop a flag for your class.

Graduation—End of School

Depending on when your school starts, graduation and the end of school before summer vacation will occur at different times. Connecting with other schools to compare graduation and end-of-school routines would be a wonderful year-end project. Holding a virtual debate about a "hot topic" related to graduation or end-of-year customs is another engaging way to connect and collaborate. Have your current students compose letters for your incoming students to include words of wisdom, bits of advice, or descriptions of their favorite activities from their school year.

Summer Projects

Summer is a chance for educators to recharge their batteries and plan ahead for the coming school year. It is also a time to reflect on the activities that took place the previous school year and on ways to improve and expand on them. Analyze each connection you had your students make. Review the exit slips of learning your students created after taking part in the Mystery Location Calls. Shore up the weak points and try to come up with new ways to expand your students' learning outside the walls of your classroom. Start preparing more strategies to engage your students in connecting with others.

With more free time available during school vacations, attending conferences, **edcamps**, or **webinars** gives you the opportunity to connect with other educators. Not only can teachers gain ideas, but these can also lead to possible class calls and collaboration. Making connections and building a viable PLN will make it easier to find other classes all around the world with which to share learning adventures. Twitter brought this group of authors together, and we feel it is a great vehicle to use to build your own personal learning network and help you connect your students to collaborations around the world. However, do not neglect other ways to expand your network. Reach out to others on Facebook, LinkedIn, and other forms of social media.

Teaching summer school also gives you additional chances to connect students to experts and other classes. Try out some new ideas and seek suggestions from the students on ways they would like to connect with other students across the world. Put these ideas in a Google Doc and let other educators, students, and parents give their input.

Summer Learning

Before school ends, have your students work in groups to determine different ways that they can keep learning during the summer. Each group should develop a menu of activities. Have the children plan field trips to interesting places in their community or city. Students have to plan the trip by determining how to get to the place, the costs associated with it, refreshments, and learning outcomes.

When Paula Naugle attended Maker Camp: Blasting Off With Buzz Aldrin and a NASA virtual field trip On her summer vacation, she was so excited to have a chance to "hang out" with Buzz Aldrin that she shared the information with her previous students through their Edmodo group. She also shared the information with parents of both previous and incoming students by posting the information and link to this event through various social media sites such as Facebook and Twitter. Several of her students did attend this Google On Air Event. Google On Air is now YouTube Live. There are many different ways to share a learning experience over the summer if a teacher chooses to do so. You can also record the session and save it for when you are back together with your students in the fall.

Summer Reading

Many public libraries have summer reading programs. Check to see if your local library has such a program and have your students help get the word out about it to their peers. Allow students to come up with their own suggested list of reading materials (books, magazines) they recommend. They can create such lists on their tech devices and can use **QR codes** to show their ratings and comments on books. Also, consider recording yourself reading a chapter book to have students follow along during the summer months. Pick a book that can be fun or interesting to your students and record yourself reading the chapters. You can easily share the videos with students via Google Classroom or, if you are comfortable enough, create a YouTube channel.

If you had your students on Edmodo or Google Classroom during the school year, you may want to set up a summer reading group within Edmodo or Google Classroom, as was done by several teachers we know. Not only can your students join, but you can share the code with other classes you have connected with during the school year, and have them join in the summer reading fun too! We have found that the students love staying connected to each other during the summer. The teachers can post book reviews and discussion questions for virtual book clubs, and students can write reviews of books they read over the summer.

Notes

1. www.yollisclassblog.blogspot.com/2012/02/mardi-gras-learning-from-experts.html.
2. www.plpnetwork.com/2012/05/29/our-skype-adventures-creating-connected-learners-in-the-global-classroom/.
3. For more information about the series visit www.livingmath.net/Reviews/Reviews-ChildrensMathLit/SirCumferenceSeries/tabid/414/Default.aspx.
4. www.virtualvisittours.com/category/castles-northern-ireland/.
5. www.baseballhall.org/education/distance-learning.
6. www.yadvashem.org/yv/en/museum/virtual_tour.asp.
7. www.earthdaybags.org.

8. www.sites.google.com/site/environmentalheroesquest/home.
9. www.dogonews.com/2013/5/6/may-is-national-inventors-month.

Resources

April Fools' Day: www.cybraryman.com/april.html
Arbor Day: www.cybraryman.com/plants.html
Autism: www.cybraryman.com/autism.html
Baseball: www.cybraryman.com/baseball.html
Castles Northern Ireland, Virtual Visit Tours: www.virtualvisittours.com/category/castles-northern-ireland/
Cinco de Mayo: www.cybraryman.com/cincodemayo.html
Coping Strategies: www.cybraryman.com/coping.html
Earth Day: www.cybraryman.com/environment.html
End of School Year and Graduation: www.cybraryman.com/endofschool.html
Exit Slips: www.cybraryman.com/exitslips.html
Father's Day: www.cybraryman.com/fathersday.html
Flag Day: www.cybraryman.com/flagday.html
Holocaust: www.cybraryman.com/holocaust.html
Humor: www.cybraryman.com/humor.html
Inventors: www.cybraryman.com/scientists.html
Learning and Baseball: www.cybraryman.com/baseballlearning.html
Makerspaces: www.cybraryman.com/makerspaces.html
Mardi Gras: www.yollisclassblog.blogspot.com/2012/02/mardi-gras-learning-from-experts.html
Memorial Day: www.cybraryman.com/memorialday.html
Mother's Day: www.cybraryman.com/mothersday.html
Passion-Based Learning: www.cybraryman.com/passionbasedlearning.html
Pi Day: www.cybraryman.com/math.html
Standardized Testing: www.cybraryman.com/standardizedtests.html
St. Patrick's Day: www.cybraryman.com/stpatrick.html
Summer: www.cybraryman.com/summer.html
Summer Learning: www.cybraryman.com/summerlearning.html
Summer Reading: www.cybraryman.com/summerreading.html
Summer School: www.cybraryman.com/summerschool.html
Teaching the Holocaust: www.npr.org/blogs/ed/2015/02/20/387654149/teaching-the-holocaust-new-approaches-for-a-new-generation
Women's History: www.cybraryman.com/women.html

The Next Chapter

In Chapter 6 we will explore ways to go on virtual field trips. We will also look at a few of the adventures that we have done. This chapter will explore ways to find other virtual field trips.

6

Virtual Field Trips Revisited

Virtual field trips have changed drastically over the last five years since the first edition of *Connecting Your Students with the Virtual World* came out. The rapid change in technology has allowed educators to access field trips to places where you never were able to take your students before. If you have the technology capabilities you can take students on a simple virtual field trip on a project, screen, and computer to immerse students into a new world with virtual glasses. The changing landscape of technology in education has the ability to create new possibilities for students. High school students can now visit colleges across the country without even having to fly and bear a large expense before they even decide if they want to attend the school. Teachers can explore the Grand Canyon with students or take a virtual tour of NASA. Virtual field trips bring more depth to social studies and other subjects.

In this chapter, we will explore ways to take your students on adventures outside the classroom by taking advantage of virtual field trips (VFTs). There are so many wonderful virtual learning opportunities that can help your students gain knowledge in all subject areas. They can explore and learn about the world without leaving their classroom. Unfortunately, because of cutbacks and the demands of testing, many schools do not provide their students with the opportunity to take actual field trips, so virtual field trips can bring valuable learning to your students. We strongly feel that taking students on actual field trips to explore their community, town, city, or state are great learning experiences. If you are fortunate enough to go on a field trip in person, you can easily share your trip via FaceTime, Skype, or Google Meet with other classes while you are at the site. In this way the students sitting in their classrooms could go along on your adventure too. You can also record the trip and then share it later with other classes.

Jerry used to enjoy taking his classes on trips to historical sites, museums, and office and work sites. One of his all-time favorite trips was to see the Tuskegee Airmen at the Fantasy of Flight Museum in Polk City, Florida, thanks to Dennis Dill (@DennisDill). As a result of tweeting about that event, he found that one of his followers was also in the audience; Diana Rendina (@DianaL-Rendina) had chaperoned her class from Tampa. It is also a good idea to have your students complete a learning page for either an actual or a virtual field trip. This can be done by using an online survey or a paper form. The main learning features of participating in the trip should be covered. If you are able to take a trip outside your school building, please have your students help plan the trip. They can help determine how you will get to the site and costs involved; also have them prepare some pre-trip information about the place you are visiting.

Examples of Successful Virtual Field Trips

We provide examples of virtual field trips that we might have taken with our class along with sharing ideas from our PLN. Some of these trips are as simple as bringing in an Eagle Cam to watch bald eagles, and some of the ideas involve exploring a museum virtually. Our hope is that these give you some simple ideas to help enhance lessons with your students in the classroom.

Decorah Eagle Cam

One winter, Paula learned about the Decorah Eagle Cam[1] from Nancy Carroll's blog post "Teachable Moment—Watch Live—Iowa Eagles."[2] The next day Paula had her students viewing the live stream. The excitement generated by watching this live feed spread throughout our building and community, and soon everyone was talking about it. I wrote about paying it forward on my blog.[3] We checked on the eagles daily and were thrilled to witness the hatching of the eggs. We were sad when the last eaglet was old enough to fledge the nest. However, each year starting in February, the Decorah eagles become a part of our classroom and we share things we observe with others during video calls.

If you visit explore.org you will not only find the Decorah eagles but over 100 public broadcasts of live streams of animals in their natural habitats. Explore allows for educators to bring in animals to the classrooms as students are learning about a habitat or ecosystem. The best part is that the website is free to access and easy to navigate.

Virtual Trip to Liberty State Park and the Intrepid Air and Space Museum

In the spring of 2012, Billy started to explore and expanded beyond the Mystery Location Call and took Nancy Carroll's class with him on his field trip. Eight years later, the ability to visit places has changed. You can now take virtual tours of many of the national parks through the National Parks website, along with some amazing lesson plans: www. nps.gov/teachers/index.htm. You can explore the Statue of Liberty or even Ellis Island as Billy was able to take Nancy's class on tour using his smartphone. Check out these fantastic virtual tours: www.nps.gov/ teachers/index.htm and www.nps.gov/elis/learn/photosmultimedia/ virtual-tour.htm. The National Park Service is a great jumping-off point to take students on virtual field trips. All you need to get started is Internet access and a computer.

Take the journey with us as we explore how Billy, who teaches in New Jersey, took a class from Massachusetts on a virtual tour of the Statue of Liberty, Ellis Island, and the Intrepid Air and Space Museum.

In the spring of 2012, Billy started to experiment with going beyond the Mystery Location Call. The fourth-grade students at Beatrice Gilmore Elementary School in New Jersey were headed to Ellis Island and the Statue of Liberty for their school field trip. Nancy Carroll (in Massachusetts) and Billy had been in contact and playing with ideas of how to connect beyond the Mystery Location Call. Back then they were just using Skype. In Chapter 4 we learned one way in which Nancy and Billy took their Mystery Location Call further by learning about Indianapolis and had their fun with Super Bowl XLVI. Now you might be saying to yourself, well, that is a pretty fun way of expanding the Mystery Location Call; but Nancy and Billy took it a step farther.

Nancy's class was studying Ellis Island and just happened to finish the unit. Prior to the field trip Billy and Nancy discussed a possible Skype call during the field trip depending on connectivity. Billy attempted to make a Skype call and was able to get through to bring Ellis Island virtually to Nancy's class in Massachusetts. This call lasted about 15–20 minutes through Billy's cell phone. The students in Massachusetts were able to see the different places at Ellis Island as Billy ran around showing them the Great Hall, the Registry Room, the Statue of Liberty, and the American Immigrant Wall of Honor. The students also were able to see the building of the "Freedom Tower," as it is visible from Ellis Island (Figures 6.1 & 6.2).

Scholastic offers a great interactive tour of Ellis Island as well if you cannot make the trip in person or don't have a class with which to connect.[4] The National Park Service also offers a virtual field trip to Ellis Island, part of Statue of Liberty National Monument.[5] If you are looking for some information about the history of Ellis Island, make sure to visit "Ellis Island—Facts & Summary" on history.com and Jerry's Cybrary Man site.[6]

In the spring of 2013, Billy again took Nancy's class on a VFT with his fourth-grade class. This year the students at Beatrice Gilmore Elementary School visited the Intrepid Air and Space Museum for a guided tour. The students in Massachusetts were able to learn about the Intrepid along with the students in New Jersey. They were even able to look up pictures on the Internet about the planes the guide was talking about.

Figure 6.1 View of the Freedom Tower Being Constructed

Figure 6.2 View of Ellis Island From the Boat

Connected Classrooms: Explore the Tundra With Polar Bears International and Discover Education

Who doesn't love polar bears? Discover Education is another amazing site that offers a ton of free virtual field trips. Billy has participated in the webinars a number of years ago and found the webinar to be very informative. When Tundra With Polar Bears International first started, it was a collaborative effort between the Google Maps team and Polar Bears International.[7] It took place in Churchill, Manitoba, one of the world's best places to see polar bears. Check out the virtual field trip here: www.discoveryeducation.com/learn/tundra-connections/.

Dennis Dill in Florida (@DennisDill) Connects His Students With South Africa

Dennis Dill describes his collaborative experience:

> *By definition collaboration is the action of working with someone to produce or create something and it seems as though it has become an education buzzword embraced by many to illustrate how we are assisting kids into becoming college and career ready, but is this the only way to view this action?*
>
> *I had the opportunity to connect with George Hasani, a Principal at a K-12 school in South Africa when he visited my school in the United States with a group of his students. After a conversation about his students' and*

staff's needs and wants we saw an opportunity to assist. We wanted to help him with professional development for his staff and create an enhanced learning environment for his students. The enhancement is not coming in the form of teachers from the United States teaching them, but through students in the United States connecting and assisting in their learning . . . Collaboration with a Purpose.

Collaboration with a Purpose views collaboration not as just completing a project, but rather making a difference. This is a bit different than working with people and planting some trees and making a difference in the environment, which is a great project, but this collaboration is making a tangible difference in a person's life. In this case, my students will be working with students in South Africa and there will be the requisite cultural exchange, which will benefit both parties, but the change shift happens when this interaction turns into conversational English tutoring. Yes, there will be collaborative projects, but the outcomes or goals of the project are different for each student. From the South African perspective, it is to learn English, Math, and Science through interacting with American students, but from the American perspective each South African student is a collaborative project.

We have a couple of different ways we connect. We try to connect regularly via Skype, but with the seven hour time difference and different school schedules it makes it challenging.

Student-Created Virtual Field Trips

With the technology tools available today, have your students create their own virtual field trips to historical sites or interesting things in your community, town, or city. Google has a website called Tour Creator where students or educators can create their own tour or even take a tour. Imagine creating a tour of your school (make sure if you include any pictures of students that you have signed permission forms). You can also develop a VFT of your school to share and compare with other classes. Divide the class up for this project and assign students jobs as in the Mystery Location Call.

Some Suggested Jobs:

- ◆ *Project manager* oversees the entire operation and ensures all students are working on their jobs.
- ◆ *Site selectors* choose interesting places in the community, town, or city to do this project.
- ◆ *Researchers* gather interesting material on the site.
- ◆ *Script writers* choose the wording that will be used in the production.

- *Scenery locators* select interesting places to film the production.
- *Videographers* are the team of students who will capture the trip on film.
- *Tech map coordinators* make use of Google Maps and Google Earth to create visuals (see the next subsections).
- *Hosts* are on air and will introduce the project and take us through it from beginning to end.
- *Sound and visual engineers* do checks to make sure the quality of the audio is clear and good.
- *Evaluators* view the project before it is released and make suggestions to improve the project.

Once the project is complete, you can then share it with classes that you have connected with in other states or countries.

Google Maps, Earth, Google Lit Trips, and Google Arts & Culture

Google Maps is a great way to explore different locations. "Google Maps for Education provides resources to help teachers and students explore, create, and collaborate with mapping tools. Students who are taught geography are better equipped to understand how human and physical systems interact and to make informed decisions based on that knowledge."[8] Visit the Liwa Desert, North East through Google Camel View.[9] Google also offers some fantastic street views of famous locations from around the world.[10] We suggest downloading Google Earth to explore other lands as well.

Are you exploring or studying the oceans? Then this a must visit: Google Maps' Street View, Oceans offers an interactive guide through the underwater world of the oceans.[11]

If you are learning about different art museums, make sure you visit the website of the Google Cultural Institute and take tours of all the different art museums from around the world.[12]

Google Lit Trips allows a reader to integrate the technology of Google Earth with places visited by characters in a novel.[13] The Google Lit Trip site has files you download and run in Google Earth, which contain placemarks of places cited in that particular book. The placemarks can also contain supplementary material, including photos, videos, discussion questions, and links to other sites that allow the reader to "get into the book." You can also build your own Google Lit Trip and share it with others. Imagine having your class collaborate with one or more classes to create a Google Lit Trip based on a novel read by all. Google has also made it easy to visit Art Museums and learn about culture centers. Take a look at https://artsandculture.google.

com/ to find out about what programs you can museums or artists your class can learn about.

Museum Virtual Trips and Historical Sites

Many museums now offer virtual visits to their museums, and they are free. All you need is an Internet connection and a computer or a device that has web browsing capabilities. Imagine a class in Anytown, USA, can now take a trip to the Louvre or the Museum of Natural History. All these trips can now take place through virtual trips. Check out these few museums and search for museums you are interested in:

- ◆ Louvre: www.louvre.fr/en/visites-en-ligne
- ◆ Museum of Natural History: https://naturalhistory.si.edu/visit/ virtual-tour
- ◆ Seven Wonders of the World: www.panoramas.dk/7-wonders/ colosseum.html
- ◆ The White House: www.whitehouse.gov/about-the-white-house/ the-white-house/

Imagine discussing the battle of Gettysburg and taking your students to the battlegrounds. Or going to visit the Liberty Bell or a rain forest. The Internet has changed the landscape of education and now through modern technology you can take students to all of these wonderful sites. Most of the sites have virtual tours that you can find by simply searching for them. Check out https://historyview.org/ as well, but make sure you check the site before any advertising and make sure the site will load on your school district site.

During the pandemic, Rob Pennington, a principal Billy knows in Connecticut, designed a virtual field trip for his students as they could not visit Boston on their scheduled field trip. Check out Rowayton's Breakout of Boston Trip: https://sites.google.com/norwalkps.org/rowaytons-virtual-boston-field/home. The virtual trip that Rob designed is another idea that could be designed for students. Make sure you also search for similar trips as there might be something out there already!

Notes

1. Decorah eagles, Ustream.TV, www.ustream.tv/decoraheagles.
2. www.teachingiselementary.blogspot.com/2011/04/teachable-moment. html.

3. A teachable moment—pay it forward, Ms. Naugle's Classroom Blog, www.pnaugle.blogspot.com/2011/04/teachable-moment-pay-it-for ward.html.
4. Ellis Island interactive tour with facts, pictures, video, Scholastic.com, www.teacher.scholastic.com/activities/immigration/tour/.
5. www.nps.gov/elis/learn/education/learning/scholastic-virtual-field-trip.htm.
6. www.history.com/topics/ellis-island; www.cybraryman.com/immigra tion.html.
7. https://plus.google.com/u/0/events/ccf8j1o7l92dkr43826tai21ov8.
8. Education, Google Maps, www.maps.google.com/help/maps/education/.
9. www.goo.gl/x37vuf.
10. www.google.com/maps/views/u/0/home?gl=us.
11. www.google.com/maps/views/u/0/streetview/oceans?gl=us.
12. www.google.com/culturalinstitute/u/0/project/art-project.
13. www.googlelittrips.com/GoogleLit/Home.html.

Resources

Bringing Social Studies to Life: www.teachhub.com/bringing-social-stud ies-life
Explore Plimoth Plantation: www.plimoth.org/learn
Field Trips: www.cybraryman.com/fieldtrips.html
Google: www.cybraryman.com/google.html
Kids as Tour Guides: Integrating Student-Created Media into History Class: www.edsurge.com/n/2015-02-20-kids-as-tour-guides-integrating-stu dent-created-media-into-history-class
Kiker Symbaloo: www.sites.google.com/site/kikerlearning/google-dash board
North America Virtual Field Trips: www.discoveryeducation.com/ northamerica/event.cfm
This Land Is Your Land: www.oiadaintl.org/
Virtual Tours and Field Trips: www.theteachersguide.com/virtualtours. html#Museums

The Next Chapter

In Chapter 7 we will explore ways to connect through games and esports. We will discuss different collaboration games that can be used in the classroom and discuss the new esports part of the education world.

7

Connecting Through Games and Esports

Games Are Changing the Education Landscape

We cannot escape the fact that for many of our students, video and other games are a big part of their lives. Video games especially have come a long way and are now much nicer in terms of graphics and action and they are more engaging. Observing my youngest granddaughter, who is eight, interacting with others is very interesting. She has formed groups and teamed up with others. She is improving her language and communication skills and she is learning a lot from other game participants. She works patiently and calmly, working through problems and attaining her game goals. Of course, her parents and I are making sure she is a good digital citizen.

Video games challenge students in adventures that have them solve problems and keep them engaged. They are having fun, gaining confidence, and they are not afraid to make mistakes while seeking to go to the next level.

In a recent article in Psychological Bulletin, *Benoit Bediou and his colleagues (2018) reviewed all of the recent research (published since 2000) they could find concerning the cognitive effects of playing action video games. Their analysis of the correlational studies revealed, overall, strong positive relationships between the amount of time gaming and high scores on tests of perception, top-down attention, spatial cognition, multitasking, and cognitive flexibility (ability to switch strategies quickly when old ones strategies don't work).*[1]

Gaming and Global Collaboration by Steve Isaacs @mr_isaacs

Gaming is definitely a common language among students. Kids around the world are playing games, watching others play games, and seeking opportunities to play and learn together. This is a very powerful approach to learning as it is truly meaningful to our students. I teach game design and development and feel that it is important for students to collaborate with other students as well as industry professionals. I am happy to report that game developers, YouTube creators, and others in the field have been very supportive when it comes to sharing their experiences with my students. This has taken several forms. On many occasions, we have invited a guest speaker to join us via video conferencing. Microsoft Education has an annual event called Global Skype-a-thon. When I first heard of it I figured this was a great opportunity to capitalize on this idea of focusing on bringing professionals into my classroom. It has been a huge success and we have met with dozens of professionals. It is so important for students to hear the experiences of those in the field to truly understand what the industry is like and what is involved in different jobs in the field. We have had professional Minecraft builders join us, YouTube influencers, game designers (digital and non-digital), audio engineers, and many more. We are lucky that current technology makes this easy. Many professionals are willing to dedicate 30 minutes to speak to a class from their home or office where face-to-face meetings would certainly present different challenges.

In addition to guest speakers, we have had a few opportunities to work more closely with industry professionals. I provide a lot of choice in terms of what tools my students use to create their projects. As a result, it is not realistic to think that I am going to be the expert when it comes to these tools. This puts a lot of responsibility for learning in the hands of my students. On several occasions we have been able to receive mentoring from someone with expertise in a given tool. There was one situation where my students wanted to develop a game in Unity and I was able to set them up with a game developer who was willing to work with them through email and occasional video conferencing during school. Another wonderful opportunity we had was when a company, Xennial Digital, wanted to work with students as advisors/partners in the creation of VR content for education. We had a group of students who worked directly with Xennial Digital as well as another school that we worked directly with. Students were able to participate in research, team meetings, and even develop and modify content.

It is also important to look at opportunities for students to collaborate with other students in and outside of the classroom. Game design lends so well to working together in design teams so that is always a focus of the class. In terms of global projects, one of our best experiences was brought to us thanks to Ben Kelly, an amazing educator in Canada. Ben developed a project called the Sustainability Shuffle, a global Minecraft project that focused on the Sustainable Development Goals. During the school year, 20 schools around the world participated and each school had the world for two weeks to create solutions to real problems to contribute to addressing the SDGs. This was one example of many that provide students with opportunities to collaborate with others through games. Games are so meaningful to kids and allow them to demonstrate their expertise in ways that other school activities often don't.

Connecting Students to Share the Learning With Quizizz Live by Heidi Samuelson, @swampfrogfirst and Mark Nechanicky, @MarkNechanicky

What Is Quizizz?

Quizizz provides free self-paced quizzes that allow students to engage with content from the classroom or at home using any device: web browser, iOS, Chrome apps, and Androids. Teachers can search for ready-made or create their own quizzes to share with their students to review or assess skills in many subject areas. Quizizz games can be played live, assigned for independent play, or shared as a practice game.

Some Advantages of Quizizz

First, when using Quizizz, students can see the questions on their device. On Kahoot, the teacher either has to project the questions or share their screen with students. Second, quizzes on Quizizz are self-paced. Third, Quizizz has a read aloud feature for questions and answer options for students.

How Do You Host a Quizizz Live to Connect Students to Share the Learning?

Using social media such as Twitter and Instagram, we share a post asking for other teachers to have their classes join our Quizizz for a certain day and time. Fifteen minutes prior to the live event, the Quizizz code is shared with the participating teachers so they can share it with their students. The students join and are able to work on a quiz on Quizizz either individually or as a member of random teams.

Nearpod Ways to Engage Students by Krista Ray

An engaged classroom starts with an empowered teacher. Nearpod is an instructional platform that merges formative assessment and dynamic media for collaborative learning experiences. The benefits of Nearpod are many. With Nearpod teachers capture student understanding at every moment. Sync interactive lessons across student devices and get in the moment insights into each student learning. It is built for any teacher; any classroom, anywhere.

Teachers can upload and intuitively tech-enhance their existing Power-Point presentations and Google Slides into interactive lessons or they can choose from a library of customizable, standards-aligned, K–12 lessons. Then, teachers launch on any device, operating system or tech environment. With Nearpod, teachers will be using a technology that fuels connection by making digital learning dynamic and collaborative with the immersive activities and formative assessments like virtual reality and game-based quizzes delivered through one seamless learning experience.

Teachers will be searching and customizing 7,500+ pre-made lessons for every subject and grade level. Nearpod works with trusted educational partners to empower teachers to create and deliver engaging digital learning experiences. Visit nearpod.com for a full list of educational partners. Schools and districts have the option of including premium content packages to meet unique needs such as digital citizenship and literacy, social emotional learning, English learners, college and career exploration, historical perspectives and literacy, and learning labs professional development.

Teachers love using Nearpod to create and deliver interactive digital learning experiences, and with a school or district license, they can do even more. With a school or district license to Nearpod, you unlock more media and assessment features. You will have nine formative assessments and 12 media types, including Desmos graphs and the student notes feature. With a student of district license, teachers experience unlimited storage, larger class sizes, multiple active sessions, and Nearpod for sub-plans. A few other great benefits to a school or district license to Nearpod is the ability to integrate with LMS tools such as Canvas, Schoology, Blackboard, and Google Classroom. And, the user management interface is enhanced with an administrator usage reporting dashboard.

When lessons are in Nearpod, the same learning can happen in school and at home. We know many schools and districts have been tasked with being flexible with their instruction. With Nearpod, teachers can "Nearpodize" any resource or teach a pre-made lesson. They can upload their existing resources, or use our Google Slides add-on to quickly enhance lessons with Nearpod.

And, then they can choose to teach synchronously or asynchronously with our live or student paced options. Nearpod is the perfect fit for traditional in-classroom teaching, a hybrid model, or completely remote.

Esports in Education

Esports is becoming very popular in education as it is starting to become popular across the world. Next you will find a success story shared by a member of our PLN, Chris Aviles.

SUCCESS STORIES

Creating and Connecting Communities With Esports?
by Chris Aviles

In September 2018, after six months of planning, my school district approved the creation of my FH Knights esports team. The FH Knights are the first middle school esports team in the country. We are currently taking on all-comers in Rocket League. I say all-comers because as the first middle school esports team in the country, there were no other middle schools to play, so I scheduled colleges. For our first match, I reached out to Rutgers University to see if they would play us. To my surprise, they agreed. The first middle school esports match ever wasn't against another middle school, it was against a college.

While I originally scheduled Rutgers for the competition, I quickly realized an amazing, unintended consequence. After the match I overheard my students talking about the Rutgers team. Who were they? What were they like? What is college esports like? By playing Rutgers, my students became interested in learning more about college life and the college kids on the other side of the computer. I knew I had to tap into that curiosity.

Playing colleges has become an important part of my esports program. For the last three seasons, I have scheduled my middle schoolers to play against colleges all over the state. After the match, I set up a call between my kids and the college kids. Everyone introduces themselves, the college students talk about what they're majoring in, and then my kids get to ask questions about college life and esports. Students on my team who may have not seen themselves as going to college are now making plans on what college they want to attend and what esports team they want to join.

Connecting my students with college players in New Jersey has been powerful. As my esports program has grown, we've been able to help other middle schools start esports programs. Our schedule grew from only playing colleges to having our own middle school esports league with over 30 teams. The Garden State Esports (GSEsports.org) league isn't just for New Jersey middle schools. Any middle school from around the country can join our league because there is value in connecting students with esports teams from different parts of the country.

In esports, it can be easy to treat your opponent poorly because you can't actually see them. They're playing behind a screen and anonymity can sometimes lead to hostility. That's why I've instituted a "virtual handshake" after matches. Similar to when we play colleges, after a match against another middle school esports team we will "shakes hands" via video call. That way students can see their opponent and realize they're real people, just like them. Further, students generally tend to get curious about their opponents. Players will ask each other where they're from and what it is like to live where they live. Connecting students with other middle schoolers in-state and from around the country has helped my students realize that kids like them are leading interesting lives around the country. I think connecting students through esports helps them realize they're part of a caring community of gamers that, despite distance, are ready, willing, and able to connect with them. My students have shared gamer tags with opponents and turned them into new friends by adding them to their friend list!

Note

1. "Benefits of Play Revealed in Research on Video Gaming," *Psychology Today*. www.psychologytoday.com/us/blog/freedom-learn/201803/benefits-play-revealed-in-research-video-gaming.

Resources and Sites

Benefits of Play Revealed in Research on Video Gaming | Psychology Today. https://www.psychologytoday.com/us/blog/freedom-learn/201803/benefits-play-revealed-in-research-video-gaming
Kahoot: https://kahoot.com/
"Teachers, students, businesses, and parents all use Kahoot for group learning, e-learning, distance learning, and self-study everywhere. Host a live game with questions or a quiz on a big screen or share with remote players."

Kahoot page: www.cybraryman.com/kahoot.html
Quizizz: https://quizizz.com/

"Free tools to teach and learn anything, on any device in person or remotely. Use Quizizz for distance learning. Build community and keep everyone engaged—even if you're not in the same place!"

Quiz and Test Generators page: https://cybraryman.com/quiz.html
Quizlet: https://quizlet.com/

"From flashcards to help you learn *français*, to games that make it easy to get a handle on history, use a variety of tools to conquer any challenge. Each new thing you learn is an achievement. Quizlet breaks down topics and subjects, so you accomplish something new every step of the way."

Quiz and Test Generators page: https://cybraryman.com/quiz.html

The Next Chapter

In Chapter 8 we will explore ways to connect with parents, along with a few tools to make that communication easier.

8

Connecting With Parents

Connecting with parents or guardians is an important part of the educational process. In this digital age, we now have many ways that educators can connect. We can text, call, email, or employ one of the many different applications there are for communicating with parents. Those apps include Remind, Class Dojo, and Seesaw, just to name a few. Parents and teachers can also connect via conferencing (see Chapter 2: Taking Video Conferencing to the Next Level). Teachers and parents need to work together to ensure the correct usage of technology by their children. We cannot stress enough the importance of parents monitoring their child's Internet usage and having them practice good digital citizenship. There are good netiquette and cyber safety tips with parental controls like Net Nanny and Bark. Parents need to also model good netiquette when using technology.

Connecting With Parents

It is important that teachers and schools keep in contact with parents or guardians to inform them of school happenings, their child's progress, and ways they can support each other. Regular communication helps build better relationships between parents and teachers, which will hopefully mean better academic performance and behavior of the students. We must be cognizant that parents know their children better and were their first teachers.

Teachers need to find the best way each parent would like to communicate. We have many communication channels at our disposal. In the past, most parent-teacher communication was done in person, by mail, or by the telephone. Now, we can also take advantage of digital forms of communication like emails, texts, or video conferences. Communicating today is quicker, more user-friendly, and saves time.

Some Tools to Connect

Here are some tools that we have encountered that we feel work well when communicating with parents. Feel free to check out these tools and try them out in your classroom.

- **Remind** www.remind.com/: "Millions of educators, students, and parents use Remind to connect with the people and resources that help them teach and learn. Remind is a simple and easy text app to use. It enables you to have a direct line and two-way communication between teachers, students, parents, and administrators for updates, instruction, and keeping everyone informed. You can send or schedule a text message (including attachments) to remind students and families about important due dates, upcoming tests and quizzes, schedule changes, field trips, or other pertinent information. Remind integrates with Google Drive, Microsoft OneDrive, SignUpGenius, Quizlet, and many others. Remind translates into over 90 languages. You can also share files and links."
  Jerry's Remind page: www.cybraryman.com/remind.html
- **Class Dojo** www.classdojo.com/: "This free communication platform brings teachers, parents, and students together. Teachers and students can share their amazing moments from class so parents are always part of what's happening. Teachers also use Class Dojo during remote learning times, letting them send lessons and activities to students at home."
  Jerry's Class Dojo page: www.cybraryman.com/classdojo.html
- **Seesaw** https://web.seesaw.me/: "Students use built-in annotation tools to capture what they know in Seesaw's digital portfolio. Teachers deeply understand student thinking and progress—enabling them to teach better. Families gain a window into their student's learning and engage with school happenings."
  Jerry's Seesaw page: http://cybraryman.com/seesaw.html

Monitor a Child's Internet Usage

In this day and age, it is important that parents monitor their child's Internet usage to prevent their children from encountering inappropriate, explicit, or disturbing content and to stay safe.

- **Facebook Messenger for Kids, Messenger Kids** https://messen gerkids.com/: Messenger Kids is a free video calling and messaging app for smartphones and tablets. Parents control the contact list, and kids control the fun. Keep in touch with close friends and family fun-filled features like filters and stickers.
  Jerry's Facebook page: www.cybraryman.com/facebook.html
- **Netiquette for Children**: Parents should work with their children on their online presence and usage of the Internet. Teach them how to be responsible and behave properly. Make sure they carefully watch what they write online to ensure it is not a harmful message that could hurt someone's feelings or one that can be taken the wrong way. Have them respect the privacy of others while not sharing their personal information or passwords.
  Jerry's Etiquette, Netiquette, and Social Skills page: https://cybra ryman.com/etiquette.html

Cyber Safety Tips

Parental Controls

Parent controls are tools or software that enable the ability to monitor and manage their children's Internet usage, block certain sites, limit downloads, and set the duration of time on the Internet. This is done to prevent their children from encountering malicious content, scams, false or misleading content, and keep them safe from cyberbullying.

- **Net Nanny** www.netnanny.com/: With Net Nanny®, you can monitor your family's digital habits and protect them from harmful content. Net Nanny provides the most effective content filtering to keep your family's website browsing safe in real-time.
- **Bark** www.bark.us/: Bark's affordable, award-winning dashboard proactively monitors text messages, YouTube, emails, and 30+ different social networks for potential safety concerns, so busy parents can save time and gain peace of mind.

◆ **Cyber Safety and Security Pages** http://cybraryman.com/cyber safetypages.html: Parents want to know what their children are doing in school and how they are progressing. They also want to learn how they can help their child succeed better. Teachers are trying to find out how to work with students and the best way that each child learns. Working together by communicating regularly will help improve a student's work and behavior which in turn will help them achieve more academic success.

The Next Chapter

In Chapter 9 we will explore ways our PLN has connected their classrooms. We hope that this chapter helps you gain some more valuable ideas to bring to your classroom.

9

How Will You Connect?

As we have said before, we think it is important to be able to connect your students outside of your classroom. However, we understand that not everyone is ready to connect yet. We wanted to share stories from our PLN that show ways you can either connect with other classes or find new ideas to bring into your classroom. There are many different stories from members of our PLN and these stories take place across the United States. We want you to share what your story might be and how will you connect after reading these stories.

Flat Stanley and Travel Buddies

Flat Stanley and **Travel Buddies** give students an opportunity to learn about other countries and cultures as well as to appreciate their own community and culture more. These projects connect students at first and can lead to collaboration. *Flat Stanley* was a book written by Jeff Brown, about a boy who was flattened by a bulletin board and had many adventures. The book inspired the Flat Stanley Project, in which Flat Stanley gets passed along to other classrooms and locations across the globe. Students keep track of the travels of Flat Stanley by writing letters and taking pictures of the Flat Stanleys they send to others. If you get a Flat Stanley and have to do an adventure, we would suggest the following supplies: fishing line (to hang him up), masking tape (to secure him), and a dowel stick (to hold him out at a distance for photographs).[1]

Making Connections With Flat Stanley: *Framed in France*[2]
by Meghan Everette, @bamameghan

Here is a story from one of another member of our PLN, Meghan Everette in Alabama, that was featured on the Scholastic blog.[3]

* * *

Our school took on the challenge of "Going Global" this year. Each grade is identified by a continent, and in our second year of 1:1, we are reading, learning, and connecting with places all over the globe. It's an exciting time to be in school, but often, young students aren't familiar with geography and have a hard time understanding distances as well as the cultures of places far away. Welcome familiar face Flat Stanley who helped us explore the world from our classroom!

We started the year reading *Flat Stanley* following a simple lesson plan. [See the Appendix for a lesson plan.] Last year, my students made "reading buddies" out of the Stanley template to have around the room. This year we actually put Stanley *in the mail*! Our "class Stanley" is traveling from city to city, with his adventures being recorded on a digital form. The form is linked to a Google Map so all the first grade classes can log in and see where he has gone.

The next part of the lesson plan involves the kids individually mailing off "Stanleys."

Here's what we do:

◆ Parents send in addresses of far away family or friends.
◆ Parents donate postage stamps (so I don't have to buy them).
◆ We make a paper Stanley and mail him with a letter.
◆ The letter asks for them to have an "adventure" with Stanley, take photos, and send Stanley back.
◆ The stuff we have gotten back has been great. (Grandparents have been *wonderful* about sending elaborate packages back!)

My class loves Stanley. I cut a full-size boy from insulation sheeting with a heat knife. Stanley swung from the ceiling like a kite but has now joined our class. Kids walk by and give him high-fives each day and say hello. I decided we needed to keep reading, and selected the latest Stanley story, *Framed in France,* as our next class book. Though not all my first graders are at the level where they can read the story, I have a class set to encourage them to follow along and give them a sense of autonomy over reading a chapter book. They love being able to see the pictures firsthand.

Figure 9.1 Flat Stanley and Pictures From Around the World

While reading, we created a scrapbook of our time in France with Stanley. Our books are simply four folded pages with a cardstock cover. Students folded the books. I downloaded and printed pictures and pieces we would need. Everyone was able to decorate the cover of their scrapbook with stickers and travel items. Then we added information to our book as we read each chapter. It's hard to say what they looked forward to more: reading or scrapbooking!

My students were excited and talking. I heard about plans to buy and read more Stanley adventures from the upcoming book fair. They impressed the art teacher with their knowledge of famous French artists and they have been bringing in sketches and funny versions of the *Mona Lisa*. Stanley helped make a connection to a memorable character, series of books, art, and the world through one simple and fun-to-read story.

Takeaways From Meghan's Story

Starting with something familiar and expanding it into a collaborative project is an easy way to start making global connections. Try to get your whole school involved by having each grade level participate. Reach out to the students' families (especially grandparents) to help with your project. Besides extending the reading and writing curriculum, brainstorm how to tie in the arts and STEM and have your students create an artifact to represent their global project.

Figure 9.2 Flat Stanley and Pictures From Around the World

OTHER STORIES FROM OUR PLN

Connecting With Edmodo by Kate Baker, Veteran Educator and Senior Community Engagement Manager at Edmodo

Edmodo is more than just a communication and collaboration platform with the capabilities of a learning management system that can be used anywhere learning happens—whether in person, online, or a hybrid of the two on both desktop and mobile apps. Edmodo was the hub of my ninth grade English classroom for the last ten years of my 20-year teaching career, and continues to be my central place for professional development and online community collaboration.

Edmodo provides a flexible classroom space that lets teachers and their learners connect and participate in engaging lessons, discussions, and assessments. Teachers can create private class spaces and collaborative groups with the tools needed to deliver instruction, share resources, assess learning, and facilitate discussion with such tools as small groups, scheduled and moderated classroom posts, threaded discussions, and direct messaging with parents and students. My students and I used Edmodo for our daily learning activities as they made their thinking visible with digital assignments and quizzes, but also for connecting with other classes around the world. In one such connected classroom group, called Authors' Alley, my ninth grade students in South Jersey posted working drafts of their writing in our collaborative class so that the eleventh grade AP Language and Composition students in Mrs. Krapels' class in North Jersey could provide feedback in a targeted and academic manner. As we communicated both synchronously and asynchronously, we attached links to docs and recorded screencasts to create a multi-modal experience for everyone involved. The power of this collaborative, online writing process is best exemplified with the story of my former student, Maddy, a gifted but painfully shy student who found her voice online. As we engaged in the collaborative writing process, Maddy took the initiative to also respond to her classmates, sharing her insight and creativity, and even going so far as to self-publish her own poetry in our online writing group. Maddy continued to self-publish (notice, I do not write "turn in") her own writing in the collaborative class right up until the day she graduated high school. Today, Maddy is in a creative writing program in college and I expect to see her name on the cover of published books in the future.

On Edmodo, the global community of 144 million registered users from 190 countries is just a post away. Whether participating in a global pen pal program or sharing resources with teachers around the world, Edmodo's hashtag conversations and community groups allow teachers to connect and collaborate. The Discover area of Edmodo includes high-quality educational resources, such as activities, apps, games, Edmodo Quizzes, videos, links, files, and more, shared by the Edmodo teacher community and trusted education partners. Edmodo also supports social-emotional learning with a Wellness Check tool in class spaces, a collection of social-emotional learning and teaching resources in Discover, and an app in Discover called Happy Not Perfect that provides mindfulness and relaxation exercises specific to teachers and students. Happy Not Perfect's mindfulness activities are invaluable for students and teachers who are feeling stressed. I would lead my class through a two-minute, shake-out-the-stress mindfulness exercise before exams and encouraged students to access the activities and resources at home for further reinforcement. Edmodo's Wellness Check tool and integration with Happy Not Perfect allow teachers to connect with their students and for students to reflect on their wellbeing and mental health both in the class and at home.

Platforms such as Edmodo provide teachers with the opportunity to create and cultivate online community spaces that can enhance the in-person learning experience and allow students to grow and thrive as they practice the skills taught in the classroom.

Takeaways From Kate's Story

Edmodo is a great tool for teachers who are looking for a place to collaborate with other teachers in a safe environment. As educators you are able to control a platform such as Edmodo and can make the collaboration space completely private.

Connecting Internationally for Global Collaborations by Shelly Sanchez Terrell, @ShellTerrell

In 2009, I was an American teaching English to four- to six-year-olds, teens, and adults in Germany and missed home very much as well as the teacher community I left back home in Texas. To feel more connected with others I joined Twitter and began blogging. Soon I began communicating with teachers around the world on a regular basis, which led to several global collaborations between our students.

Through these platforms I connected with an incredible kindergarten teacher based in Turkey, Özge Karaoğlu. We quickly became friends and decided to collaborate on a collaborative digital storytelling project with our young students. We decided each of our students should contribute stories and hand-drawn images about different animals and we would share with each other's classes. After planning sessions on Skype and Twiddla, we chose the educational tool Voicethread as our canvas. Voicethread is an asynchronous tool which allows students to contribute to a discussion, presentation, debate, or story in various ways—audio, text, doodling, images, and videos. We uploaded the students' pictures of their animals then recorded their voices describing what their animals were doing, thinking, and saying.

Our young learners did an incredible job and enjoyed each other's animal drawings and descriptions. They were able to participate in other cultural exchanges as well and a teacher from New Zealand contributed comments to our project. This project also motivated each of our young learner classes to practice their English, because they found the experience fun! We also believe this collaborative effort was successful for our very young learners, because:

- The children's identities are hidden, since our choice of tool allowed them to share with child-friendly avatars.
- The children were encouraged to research each other's cultures and facts about the different countries, Germany and Turkey.
- The children experienced the power of using technology to make global connections and be digital publishers.
- The parents get to see the amazing advantages of using technology in the classroom to capture their child's learning and also see their imaginations at work.
- The technology we chose was easy for both teachers, parents, and children to access and use with privacy options.

Özge and I were so proud of the collaboration that we published their work in our blogs and wikis. Teachers around the world were amazed at our young English learners' fluency and enthusiasm. The amount of incredible feedback led to us being featured co-presenters at IATEFL, a very popular international conference for English language teachers in the United Kingdom. Özge and I were able to meet in person at Harrogate, UK, and present together. We continued to use collaborative tools, such as Google Docs, Skype, Twiddla, and wikis to collaborate. Our presentation was such a hit that we were interviewed and our presentation was live streamed. Thousands of teachers around the world watched our interview and presentations.

This led to us meeting up at award ceremonies for our work and each presenting at several more conferences worldwide, such as Berlin, Paris, Istanbul, Cambridge, Manchester, Liverpool, and London. We became such great friends that I attended Özge's wedding in Turkey.

Özge and I are both edtech enthusiasts and believe in the power of digital storytelling to inspire young children to learn languages and content by being creative and using what they learn to craft meaningful stories. Our passions led to more collaborative international projects and one that lasted over five years, which was hosting two Massive Open Online Courses that lasted five weeks for over a thousand teachers worldwide on how to implement digital storytelling.

Takeaways From Shelly's Story

The key points are initially making a connection and collaboration. Through Twitter, Facebook, or other social media, you can connect, share, and learn from educators all over the world. Once you have connected you can then have your students collaborate and learn from other educators' students.

Working With the Community Public Service Announcement
by Natalie Franzi, @NatalieFranzi

We work with our students to develop skills that will help them tackle real life, but often don't give them that opportunity for application. My students had been busy all year analyzing informational text, evaluating sources, and creating claims that they supported with textual evidence. I wanted to create a project where students could combine their passion and apply these skills in a real-world situation. I also felt that it was important to connect our students to the communities that they live in to provide experiential learning experiences. With this in mind, I designed a research project focused on producing a Public Service Announcement (PSA) about a non-profit of their choice. Their goal was two-pronged, to raise awareness and change people's attitudes towards their cause while utilizing the skills that we had been honing all year long. Students chose causes that mattered to them like The Rob Dyrdrek Foundation, ASPCA Wounded Warriors Project, and the Robinhood Foundation. These real-life connections were a driving force in producing a video that mattered to each student. I also gave students a real audience. They had the opportunity to vote on the best PSA from their class period using a rubric, that would then move on to a grade-level wide assembly. The PSAs were judged by a panel of teachers and a representative from a minor league baseball team. The PSA that was selected as the overall winner was shown at a minor league baseball game that the student attended with their friends and family.

As the teacher in the classroom, I was excited that I had designed a project that incorporated key standards addressed during the school year. Students would have the opportunity to write a script using textual evidence to support their claims and create a video using images, voice-overs, and music to persuade their audience of the importance of their cause. The plan to extend this project was also to have each group conduct some type of community service related to the non-profit. I was happy with the project that I had designed and excited to see students engage in the learning.

This project became so much more than I had expected; students were thinking hard and examining what truly mattered to them. I saw students who were not engaged in our reading class meet after school with their GoPros and skateboards to capture footage for their PSA to support the Tony Hawk Foundation. I remember a phone call with a parent who thanked me.

He shared that he had never seen his child engaged or care about something so much that was school-related. While I was flattered by the phone call, it was a reminder that we need to design instructional experiences that matter to our students and connect them to their communities. Skills and content are important but mean nothing without the context of the world around us.

Takeaways From Natalie's Story

Natalie's story is about connecting her class within her community and having students work collaboratively. We have discussed throughout the chapters in this book the importance of being connected. Connection can start with something small in the community and then grow to many of the other projects we have listed throughout the book.

Sharing a Guest Speaker: Veterinarian Live*

It is important that we provide our students with opportunities to learn about different careers to help them prepare for their future. For the past several years, Billy has brought Dr. Mark Salemi of Northside Animal Hospital (www. nahnyc.com), a veterinarian who works in the community, into his classroom. The veterinarian discusses what he does for a living. He also brings several animals with him and explains how he treats them. What makes these visits so special is that Billy shares this experience with other classrooms around the country using a Google Meet. It is a great, engaging, and fun learning opportunity for everyone involved.

Bringing in a community member in person or by using technology tools like Skype or Google Meet is an easy way to start connecting beyond the walls of your classroom. Dr. Salemi is also a board of education member and wanted to give back to the school community. We highly recommend that you survey your students' parents and find out if they would be willing to share about their careers. This can be accomplished by a classroom visit in person, a visit to their work site, or a Skype call or Google Meet. Share this learning experience with other classes in other schools by connecting them as well. All you need is an Internet connection, a webcam, and a microphone. We suggest that you save these wonderful learning events and build a library to share with students who were absent, future classes, or other classes in your school or other schools.

Dr. Salemi observes,

Connecting with children by speaking to and interacting with them in a classroom setting is always a great thrill. Talking to them about what I love

Figure 9.3 Dr. Salemi Showing Students in New Jersey, New Orleans, and Massachusetts a Turtle Shell

Figure 9.4 Dr. Salemi Showing a Ferret to the Students Both in the Room and Virtually

*to do every day and seeing how they become so engaged makes it a great ex-
perience. The ability of being able to speak to children in three states at one
time through technology, now available to the schools, is a wonderful way
for the children to learn and interact with other school districts. Most of all,
the smiles and enthusiasm experienced during these video calls make these
sessions very memorable.*

Takeaways From Veterinarian Live

Sharing guest speakers can be an easy way to connect with other classrooms
via Google Meet, Skype, or whatever video platform you feel most comfortable using. Billy was able to connect with many different classes and share
his guest speaker with other classrooms. Dr. Salemi made an interactive experience for all participants during this session, and students loved learning.
Remember, connecting your classroom can be a simple project to start.

Scientists Help Science Teachers Using Social Media
by Dan Curcio, @dandanscience

Following is a story from one of the members of the Sunday night Google Hangouts, Dan Curcio from New Jersey. He discusses in a blog post
how scientists help science teachers using social media. Dan is a passionate science educator at the Community School in Teaneck, New Jersey. He
has shared amazing projects with us and has even allowed some classes to
observe and participate using either Skype or Google Meet during different
experiments.

* * *

Making connections with many individuals *"in the field"* of education over
Twitter has enhanced my professional development tenfold. I continue to
learn from so many varying perspectives and then can reflect on what I am
doing. It has helped bring some wonderful tools into my classroom as I follow the journey of others. I also have begun to follow some great scientists,
science graduate students and science writers that are actually *"in the field"*
of science. Not all, but many, of their posts have been informative and inspiring. A lot of their posts reflect the passion they have for their field of study,
which I must say has been contagious. I see how passionate some of these
professionals can be in wanting to change and benefit this world. It immediately inspires me to get into my classroom and try to spread that passion to
my students. We as science teachers can be the bridge between the possible

passion in the field to the possible passion in the class. It is our job to inspire our students into being part of the change in the world and not just watch it from afar. Unfortunately, passion can be dulled in a learning environment for students. It seems to be our job to not allow this but instead to IGNITE passion with any and all means possible. Even OUR passion for teaching science can get bogged down at times due to many expectations put upon us. Sometimes we just need HELP. This is where I think social media can actually come in handy. (It's not always about what Justin Beiber [*sic*] had for breakfast, but if that is what you want it can be.) We can connect with like-minded or different-minded individuals to help us reflect our way through. For me I have found a couple "rock stars" in the science field that in following have excited me about what I can teach. It started when I began following an amazing science teacher Adam Taylor @2footgiraffe and his awesome hashtag that connects scientists to students in a weekly chat, #scistuchat. Being involved in a couple of those Twitter chats, I have seen some of the wonderful engagement between "field" and "class"! This pushes me to find more of these professionals and somehow connect. Just knowing of the great scientists or science writers to follow on Twitter is a great start for me. Then down the road hopefully they can see the impact they can have on science teachers and more importantly students, and would even be willing to interact with us. This could lead to making authentic connections between the science field and the classroom at any age range!

I must mention two folks in the field that have recently absolutely inspired my science thinking with some exciting tweets. Alex Wild @Myrmecos, with wonderful passion and facts about entomology, confirms my lessons to students to appreciate the beauty, importance, and power of what is thought of as "ugly." David Shiffman @WhySharksMatter, with his powerful online presence, gives the deserved respect to more amazing creatures that have been sensationalized to the point of destruction! His passion for conservation gets me all riled up, which opens up great dialogue with students when *Sharknado* and *Jaws 2000 3D* are blaring through culture.

With all this said, I obviously want more of these folks in my Twitter stream as a science teacher. I know there are many more of them out there and hope they catch wind of how great their influence can be!! So, let us find them!!! I included a form that I hope will lead to a comprehensive list of scientists, researchers, writers, grad students, and science teachers that are willing to use social media and connect with each other. Selfishly, it will be a great list to benefit my enthusiasm but will hopefully spread to the many students I encounter! Please pass this on and share and share some more with all walks of life in the GLOBAL science and teaching community![4]

Takeaways From Dan's Story

Dan's story illustrates the great benefits of being a connected educator, which allows you to keep up with the latest happenings in education, network with and learn from passionate educators and other experts in your field, learn firsthand from scientists, and share lessons or activities. Making these connections with experts outside the classroom via social media will inspire and ignite your students' passion to learn more.

Using Padlet for Reading by Jennifer Regruth

Jennifer Regruth, one of the members of the Sunday night Google Hangouts, relays how her class used the **Padlet** tool to read *The Fourteenth Goldfish* for the Global Read Aloud in 2014.

* * *

The #GRA2014, Global Read Aloud is underway! We are all enjoying the book and the kids are full of ideas about what will happen next. The book has done a good job of giving us descriptions of the characters, so the students have done a great job creating predictions.

We decided to use a tool called Padlet to share our thoughts and predictions with other classrooms. I created a new Padlet and shared the link with the kids and away they went! They even figured out how to add pictures.

We connected via GHO with another classroom to share our predictions. They students loved being on camera sharing their ideas with other fourth grade students. We are looking forward to connecting with them again at the end of the book to see if our predictions were accurate. These creative kiddos were full of great ideas![5]

Takeaways From Jennifer's Story

Figure out which web tool you can use to extend a project. Creating a Padlet allows your students' work to be easily shared with others. Others can even add to your Padlet. Connecting with other classrooms that are involved in the same project allows your students to share their thoughts and ideas beyond your classroom walls.

Global Connections by Nancy Carroll

As a Digital Learning Coach, I've been finding ways that my colleagues and their students can connect globally. Besides Mystery Location Calls (which are still by far the favorites of kids and adults alike), I was able to introduce two Global Projects to my teachers this year. One you learned about in Winter Projects the #K12Valentine Project; the other project is #EpicPals.

#EpicPals is the brainchild of Sara Malchow (@smalchow). Each month, Sara creates book collections on EpicBooks and shares them via Twitter or her blog, Digital Meanderings. Teachers can find the book collection on Epic and share it with their students. Sara also shares a specific link to Padlet for each book. After reading the stories, students can go to the Padlet and create a "sticky note" with a reflection about the book or answer the guiding question. Students then take time to read the comments from those who have already posted. In this way students are connecting with a real audience.

Some second and third grade colleagues have assigned this project to their students during reading time. Students have asked their teachers if they can also work on this during their "free" time. You know when that happens you've got a winner!

I love this project because it (a) gets students reading and (b) allows them to see what others are saying about the same book they've read.

Takeaways From Nancy's Story

#EpicPals is another easy place to get started with collaboration projects. Epic-Books has a vast collection of books for students. Padlet is an easy tool to use to collaborate; it can be used to collaborate across the hall, across the globe, or even within your classroom. If your school or district has a subscription to EpicBook, try out this simple project. #EpicPals is one of many projects we have shared throughout this book, and we hope you can find a project where you can start collaborating with your class.

Conclusion: What Will Your Story Be?

First off, we want to say THANK YOU for taking the time to read through *Connecting Your Students with the Virtual World*. We hope that we gave you some easy to use projects to start collaboration projects or ways to start connecting with other educators. Being an educator today requires us to prepare our students for a rapidly changing world. How does one adequately prepare students for jobs that don't even exist yet? What skills will our students need for their futures? As John Dewey said, "If we teach today's students as we taught yesterday, we rob them of tomorrow."

Billy and Jerry encourage you, if you haven't already done so, to start building a PLN (personal learning network). Establishing a PLN is just the first step to becoming a connected educator and leads to opportunities to connect your students to the world. Today's children are constantly plugged into tech devices. It is the job of teachers to show them how to use their devices for educational purposes. Having your students collaborate is a very important skill for today's world and for job preparation.

As a reminder, when we discuss the term "connected classrooms," we mean that classrooms connect via video conferencing, GSuite, Office 365, Edmodo, or other platforms. However, almost all of these projects can be done in school without having to connect online. We know that educators might have limited technology and may not be able to connect with other classrooms, as described in some of these projects. Keep in mind you can adapt these projects to make them work for your classroom. You do not always have to connect with another classroom via video conferencing. You can connect with the classroom across or down the hall. These projects can all be adapted to meet the technology available for your class, school, and district.

Find a simple collaborative project to begin with, and try not to overthink it. Just getting started is sometimes the hardest step along the journey. We hope that you have found this book to be useful as you have gone through it. We designed the book to be a guide and reference for all educators, no matter their technological ability level. Try these activities for yourself and share them with other educators, share them with us, or share them on Twitter using #CYSwVW. Enjoy connecting and collaborating in the virtual world.

Notes

1. www.cybraryman.com/primaryed.html#FlatStanley.
2. Scholastic Teachers. (2015). Making Connections With Flat Stanley: *Framed in France. Scholastic.com*. Retrieved February 14, 2015 from www.scholastic.com/teachers/top-teaching/2014/10/making-connections-flat-stanley-framed-france.
3. Ibid.
4. www.dandanscienceman.com/scientists-help-science-teachers-using-social-media/.
5. www.brownroom18.blogspot.com/2014/10/our-padlet-for-fourteenth-goldfish.html#sthash.x3r4uDPB.dpuf.

Glossary

#4thchat (which is now #elemEDUmeet)—A Twitter chat; originally was composed mainly of fourth-grade teachers who shared ideas, lessons, and projects. The #elemEDUmeet chat is Mondays at 8:00 p.m. (EST).

100th Day of School—The 100th day of school is the opportunity to create activities based on the number 100. Schools celebrate this event at different times (see Chapter 4).

Acceptable Use Policy—Acceptable or Fair Use Policy is a set of rules on the use of technology in schools.

Animoto—Animoto is a site that creates videos from photographs.

backchannel—Backchannel is a digital conversation that happens at the same time as a face-to-face activity.

blog—A blog or weblog is an online journal or diary in which you can express your thoughts and ideas to a global audience.

body language—Body language includes the nonverbal forms of how we communicate, such as our posture, facial expressions, touch, the way we walk, stand, sit, etc.

BYOD (Bring Your Own Device)—BYOD is a trend that many schools now allow. Students can bring their own tech devices to school.

Class Dojo—This free communication platform brings teachers, parents, and students together.

close reading—Close reading asks students to really analyze text they are reading to notice the language and features that the author employs.

collaboration—Working together to accomplish a task is collaboration.

Common Core State Standards—These are a set of high-quality academic expectations in English language arts (ELA) and mathematics that define the knowledge and skills all students should master by the end of each grade level in order to be on track for success in college and career.

Commonwealth Day—Commonwealth Day is a celebration of the Commonwealth of Nations that is held on the second Monday in March.

connected educators and connected students—Being connected means using the Internet and tech tools to reach out to others to share and learn with one another.

critical thinking—Critical thinking is the ability to analyze information and come up with a reasonable conclusion.

cultural responsiveness—Cultural responsiveness is being able to include cultural references in all aspects of learning and respect the cultures of all peoples.

database—A database is a computer-generated way to store data.

deductive reasoning—A process of reasoning to reach a logical conclusion.

digital citizenship—Parents and educators need to teach children about the responsible use of technology devices and how to be a good citizen in our digital world.

digital footprint—A digital footprint is the trail of the information that you put online and that stays online.

digital literacy—To be digitally literate one has to be able to find, understand, evaluate, create, and communicate digital information.

e-book—An e-book is an electronic version of a printed book. It can consist of not only words but pictures as well. E-books can contain clickable or hypertext links to get to sites.

edcamps—Edcamps are unconferences where participants choose the topics they want to present on and can select the sessions they want to attend or lead.

Edmodo—Edmodo is a closed social learning network that allows students to connect, learn, and share safely.

Email Around the World—A project that connected classes all around the world by email.

esports—Sport competition using video games.

exit slips—At the conclusion of a lesson or project, students submit on a piece of paper what they have learned.

Facebook Messenger for Kids—Messenger Kids is a free video calling and messaging app for smartphones and tablets.

Flat Stanley—The Flat Stanley Project started in 1995 and was inspired by the book *Flat Stanley*, written by Jeff Brown. The project includes keeping track of the travels of Flat Stanley by letter-writing. Students today take pictures of Flat Stanley in different locations where they live or travel to.

Four Cs (4Cs)—The twenty-first-century skills that many people feel were most important for K-12 learners were determined to be collaboration, communication, creativity, and critical thinking. Others have also included connectivity.

gaming—Gaming has students connecting, competing, and working collaboratively with others.Games require the use of problem-solving, critical thinking, and creativity skills.

Glogster—A multimedia platform that allows students to use a variety of media to demonstrate their learning.

Google Classroom—Google Classroom enables teachers to use the myriad of Google tools such as Google Docs, Google Drive, and Gmail to have their students work on assignments, provide feedback, and communicate with them.

Google Docs—These web-based documents allow for people all over the world to simultaneously work on Word documents, spreadsheets, and forms of presentation collaboratively.

Google Meet—A free video conferencing tool that allows up to ten participants to connect, learn, and share with one another.

Google Slides—An online presentations app that allows you to show off your work in a visual way.

hashtag (#)—A hashtag is used to mark keywords or topics in a tweet or other forms of social media.

Hispanic Heritage Month—Each year from September 15 through October 15, Hispanic culture is celebrated.

hotspot—A hotspot is a location that offers Internet access over a wireless local area network.

interactive whiteboard—An interactive whiteboard (IWB) is a display connected to a computer to project the page on a screen, and students can interact with the display using the board's pen or dry erase markers.

International Dot Day—International Dot Day on September 15 is a worldwide celebration of creativity. It was inspired by the children's book *The Dot* by Peter H. Reynolds.

ISTE—The International Society of Technology in Education is the premier nonprofit organization serving educators and education leaders committed to empowering connected learners in a connected world.

Labor Day—In the United States on the first Monday in September, this day celebrates the American Labor Movement. Labor Day in many other countries is celebrated at different times.

makerspace—Makerspaces are areas set aside in libraries and schools to allow children to learn and create.

microexpressions—Observing a person's face and their expressions such as a smile or scowl can be helpful in judging their mood.

Microsoft Teams—Communication and collaboration platform that has chat and video meeting functions.

Mystery Location Call—Two or more classes in different states or countries try to find out where the other is located. The call can usually be done by Skype or Google Meet.

netiquette—Using netiquette, the online form of etiquette, means being a responsible and proper user of the Internet.

Next Generation Science Standards (NGSS)—The National Research Council (NRC), the National Science Teachers Association (NSTA), the American

Association for the Advancement of Science (AAAS), and Achieve developed the Next Generation Science Standards.

Padlet—Padlet is an online bulletin board.

personal (or professional) learning network (PLN)—A personal learning network is your collection of people that you learn and share with. A professional learning network is a group of people in your field.

photosynthesis—The conversion of light energy (sunlight) into chemical energy and storing it in the bonds of sugar.

Pi Day—On March 14 (3/14) we celebrate the ratio of the circumference of a circle to its diameter, which is approximately 3.14159, or pi.

Plimoth Plantation—Plimoth Plantation in Plymouth, Massachusetts, is a re-creation of the original settlement of the Plymouth Colony. The historical interpreters stay in the character of people living in the seventeenth century.

PowerPoint—A PowerPoint is a slide show presentation. The PowerPoint program was created by Microsoft.

QR code—Abbreviated from Quick Response Code, a QR code is the trademark for a type of matrix barcode (or two-dimensional barcode) first designed for the automotive industry in Japan. A barcode is a machine-readable optical label that contains information about the item to which it is attached.

Read Across America—March 2, Dr. Seuss's birthday, is a nationwide reading celebration that occurs every year.

Remembrance Day—Similar to Memorial Day in the United States, Remembrance Day is celebrated in Commonwealth of Nations member states to remember those who gave up their lives while serving in the armed forces.

Remind—Remind is a free, safe messaging service for teachers to communicate with students and parents via text or email.

Seesaw—This free communication platform brings teachers, parents, and students together.

September 11, 2001—On September 11, 2001, the Islamic terrorist group al-Qaeda carried out four attacks on the United States using hijacked airplanes. The World Trade Center Twin Towers in New York City were destroyed by two airplanes, the Pentagon in Washington, DC, was hit by another, and a fourth plane was downed in Pennsylvania.

Skype—A tool to use for video and voice calls as well as instant messaging and file sharing.

social media—Internet tools like Twitter, Facebook, Pinterest, and Instagram that let people share information, pictures, and ideas.

spreadsheet—A spreadsheet is an interactive, computer-generated way to organize, analyze, and store data.

Travel Buddies—Travel Buddies are objects like a paper Flat Stanley, stuffed animals, or other items that are sent to other schools.

Twitter—Twitter is a social networking platform that connects people all over the world. The basic tweet is only 140 characters long.

Twitter educational chats—There are educational chats on Twitter seven days a week for most grade levels, subject areas, interests, and states. There are chats for students, teachers, administrators, and parents.

URL—A URL is a Uniform Resource Locator or a web address.

Ustream—Ustream is a company that provides video streaming services.

video conferencing—Video conferencing enables two or more locations to communicate visually and with voice simultaneously with one another.

virtual debates—Classes in different locations carry out a debate on a topic via Skype or Google Meet.

virtual field trips (VFT)—Virtual field trips are guided educational online journeys.

VoiceThread—This is an interactive tool that allows the sharing of comments, images, and documents.

Voxer—Voxer is a messaging app for a smartphone that is similar to a walkie-talkie but also allows for text and pictures.

webcam—A webcam is a video camera attached to a computer that allows the transmission of picture and audio.

webinars—Webinars are web-based seminars transmitted using video conferencing software.

WebQuest—WebQuests are lessons where the information has been gathered from the Internet.

wiki—A wiki, similar to a blog, is a website that is a collaboration of works contributed by multiple authors.

YouTube—YouTube is a video-sharing site that provides a lot of how-to information.

Zoom—Helps schools improve student outcomes with secure video communication services for hybrid classrooms, office hours, administrative meetings, and more.

Appendix: Flat Stanley Lesson Plan

Day 1

Reading: Chapters 1 and 2

Vocabulary or Word Work

Arthur, tailor, Jeffreys, fragile

Before Reading

Set a purpose for reading—Today we will read to meet Stanley, a very interesting character. He starts out as an ordinary boy. Let's find out what happens to Stanley and if he stays as ordinary as he starts! Good readers try to remember details about the text as they continue to read more and more of the story.

After Reading

Text-Dependent Questions

What can Flat Stanley do because he is flat?

Why does Stanley's mother take him to the doctor?

What is Stanley's response when Dr. Dan asks him how he feels?

What does Dr. Dan recommend?

What does the nurse do before Stanley leaves Dr. Dan's office?

Non-Text-Dependent Questions

Stanley's brother Arthur is a little jealous of Stanley's flatness. Would you be?

Writing Response

Some people find it safer to carry on as usual after something extraordinary has happened. In the story, Stanley's mother takes him to the doctor to have him checked out. Write a paragraph describing what happens at the doctor's office.

* Send home a parent note asking for an address to mail their child's Stanley. Find an address to mail the class Stanley (one that is trusted since this one will be tracked).

© 2016, *Connecting Your Students with the World*, B. Krakower, P. Naugle and J. Blumengarten, Routledge

Day 2

Reading: Chapter 3

Vocabulary or Word Work

apologize, Encyclopedia Britannica, phases

Before Reading

Set a purpose for reading—In the story today, Arthur is starting to get a little jealous of Stanley. Stanley decides to do something nice for Arthur, but he ends up regretting it. Read to find out what happens to Stanley when Arthur thinks only of himself.

After Reading

Text-Dependent Questions

How does Stanley get in and out of rooms now that he is flat?

Where does Stanley go to visit his friend? How does he get there and back?

How does Stanley stay safe in crowds on Sunday outings?

How does Stanley use his flatness to help others?

What can you infer about Arthur when he says "Phooey!"?

Non-Text-Dependent Questions

How do you feel about Arthur taking off and leaving Stanley in the air?

Who was Arthur thinking of at that time? Have you ever had a similar situation?

Writing Response

Often, there are advantages to finding yourself in a new and different condition. Being flat allows Stanley to do some pretty unusual things. Write a paragraph relating some of the things Stanley is able to do because he is flat.

---

* Begin making a Flat Stanley for your class. Make one larger/sturdier Stanley to be mailed and tracked for the class as a whole, and allow students to make an individual Stanley.

Day 3

Reading: Chapter 4

Vocabulary or Word Work

thieves, permission, disguise, shepherdesses

Before Reading

Character—Readers think about how characters change throughout the story. How has Stanley changed or other characters changed so far? Keep looking for ways that characters change.

After Reading

Text-Dependent Questions

List two reasons the museum is hard to guard.

What was Stanley's idea to catch the crooks?

How did Stanley feel about the disguise?

How do you know?

What did the thieves think they needed when Stanley yelled for the police?

How was Stanley rewarded?

Non-Text-Dependent Questions

Were you able to make any connections to the story? (text to self, text to text, text to world)

Writing Response

Sometimes characters have to make the best of a bad situation. Stanley is flat, but it allows him to do some incredible things. Write about how Stanley got an idea to guard the museum and how he was able to help save the day.

---

* Write a class letter to go with the class Stanley on his adventure. Make a form letter for students to fill in with their information for their personal Stanley.

© *Connecting Your Students with the World*, B. Krakower, P. Naugle and J. Blumengarten, Routledge

Day 4

Reading: Chapter 5

Vocabulary or Word Work

religion, rummage, bulged

Before Reading

Character—In this chapter Arthur feels really bad for his brother. He comes up with an idea on how to help Stanley. Read the chapter to find out what Arthur does to help Stanley.

Readers think about how characters change throughout the story. How has Stanley changed or other characters changed so far? Keep looking for ways that characters change.

After Reading

Text-Dependent Questions

By the end of the story, how does Stanley feel about being flat? Why have his feelings changed?

How does Arthur comfort Stanley?

What is Arthur's good idea to help Stanley?

By the end of the story, how does Arthur's idea work out?

Non-Text-Dependent Questions

Did the story end as you expected?

Writing Response

A person facing an unpleasant situation can become discouraged and benefit from help. At the end of the story, Arthur has a good idea for helping Stanley. Write a paragraph describing Arthur's good idea. Your paragraph should tell how Arthur comes up with this idea.

---

* Mail Stanley and help students mail their Stanley as well. Show the website where visitors can upload their Stanley information to share with the class. Keep track of visits on a class map. (Note: A new website is created each year for this project; a web search should direct you to the most current one.)

Additional Writing Prompts/Discussion Questions

Imagine that Stanley is your friend in real life. Write words and phrases that would help you describe him to someone who didn't know him. (What does Stanley look like? What kind of personality does he have? What does he like to do?)

Compare and contrast Stanley with Arthur or another character in the book.

How does Arthur feel about his brother Stanley's situation? Write a paragraph about Arthur's reactions to Stanley's flatness. Be sure to include details that show how Arthur feels.

In the story, the policemen call Mrs. Lambchop a "cuckoo." The policemen apologize when they realize they have made a mistake. Mrs. Lambchop says that people should think twice before making rude remarks. The policemen think this is a good rule. Think about a good rule you think everyone should follow. Write a paragraph about a rule you think everyone should follow (Ch. 2).

In the story, Stanley Lambchop has some good ideas about how to use his changed shape to help others. Think about a time that you had an idea to help others. Write a paragraph describing a time you came up with an idea that you used to help others (Ch. 3).

Some Stanley Links

www.teachingideas.co.uk/library/books/flatstanley.htm

www.flatstanleybooks.com/

www.flatstanley.com/

Lessons adapted from www.bookpunch.com (Lesson Plan Aid for Flat Stanley)

Guided Reading Lesson Plan M: www.flatstanley.koolkidssign.com/FS2.pdf

Flat Stanley Project

Dear Families,

We are reading *Flat Stanley* in first grade. Stanley is a little boy who becomes flat. He is able to be mailed to visit a friend in another state.

We are making a Flat Stanley at school for each child to mail. Please help us by providing an address of a family member or friend for your child to mail their Stanley to.

Name: _____

Street: _____

City: _____ State: _____ Zip: _____

We will also take donations of stamps to mail our letters. If you can send a stamp or two to help get all the Stanleys in the mail, that would be appreciated!

Please return address and stamps by *Thursday*!

—The First-Grade Teachers

Dear _____,

This is my Flat Stanley. I made him after reading the book *Flat Stanley* with my first-grade class. My favorite part of the book was _____ _____. What I like best about Stanley is _____.

We are sending Stanley on an adventure around the globe. Please take some photos with Stanley and write about his adventures with you. Then return Stanley and the information to me at:

Daphne Elementary School

2307 Main Street

Daphne, AL 36526

c/o _____ in _____ 's class

Thank you for helping me with the project. I hope you and Stanley have fun together!

Sincerely,

_____

Original Mailing: September 8, 2014

Dear Friends,

Our class has read *Flat Stanley*. Poor Stanley was flattened when a bulletin board fell on him. The good news is now he can travel the world in an envelope. Please spend some time with Stanley and take some pictures of your adventures together. **Then visit http://goo.gl/WVeOWA and upload what you have done.** We will add you to our virtual interactive map and see where Stanley has gone on his travels.

When you are done, **please send Stanley on to another location** so the adventure can continue! Include this letter so they will have directions on what to do with Stanley. You can see where Stanley has been on our map at https://goo.gl/maps/mL5jg.

If you want to share other items with us, you can mail us at:

Daphne Elementary School

c/o Meghan Everette, 1st Grade

2307 Main Street

Daphne, Alabama 36526

If you have other questions, please email Mrs. Everette at meverette@ bcbe.org and we'd be happy to tell you more. Thank you for helping our first-grade classes travel around the world this year!

Sincerely,

_____

Resources

Bibliography of Resources

Avery, S. (2011, June 14). Mystery Skype—Who Could it Be? *The Avery Bunch* [Blog post]. Retrieved from www.mravery.edublogs.org/2011/06/14/mystery/

Badura, C. (2012, January 10). When Are We Gonna Do that Again? *Comfortably 2.0* [Blog post]. Retrieved from www.craigbadura.com/2012/01/when-are-we-gonna-do-that-again.html

Blumengarten, J. (2013, March 1). *@cybraryman Read Across the States* [Video file]. Retrieved from www.youtube.com/watch?v=zxi71A_lvME

Framework for 21st Century Learning. (2011, March). *The Partnership for 21st Century Skills*. Retrieved from www.p21.org/our-work/p21-framework

Graham, J. (2014, February 3). Super Bowl ad for Microsoft Features Irvine Classroom. *The Orange County Register*. Retrieved from www.ocregister.com/articles/bedley-600029-students-microsoft.html

Hart, T. (2014, February 19). 1st Mystery Skype! *Resources from the "Hart"* [Blog post]. Retrieved from http://blogs.henrico.k12.va.us/trhart/2014/02/19/1st-mystery-skype/

Kemp, C. (2014, November 16). What Is Mystery Skype? 7 Steps to Get Started! *Mr. Kemp* [Blog post]. Retrieved from www.mrkempnz.com/2014/11/what-is-mystery-skype-8-steps-to-get-started.html

Krakower, B. (2013, February 20). Connecting Beyond the School Walls: Mystery Location Call. *Billy Krakower* [Blog post]. Retrieved from www.billykrakower.com/blog/connecting-beyond-the-school-walls-mystery-location-call

Miller, G. (2013, April 18). Try a Mystery Skype: Here's Why. *Educational Leadership in the 21st Century* [Blog post]. Retrieved from www.gregmillerprincipal.com/2013/04/18/try-a-mystery-skype-heres-why/

#MysterySkype. *Skype in the Classroom* [Website]. Retrieved from https://education.skype.com/mysteryskype

Ripp, P. (2013, February). Where in the World Are They? Students Find Out with Mystery Skype. *Leading and Learning*, 40 (5), 30–31. Retrieved from www.learningandleading-digital.com/learning_leading/201302#pg32

Scholastic Teachers. (2015). Making Connections with Flat Stanley: Framed in France. *Scholastic.com*. Retrieved from www.scholastic.com/teachers/top-teaching/2014/10/making-connections-flat-stanley-framed-france

Skype in the classroom. (n.d.). *Projects* [Website]. Retrieved from https://education.skype.com

Solarz, P. (2014, August). How to Set Up and Run a Mystery Skype Session. *What's Going on in Mr. Solarz' Class?* [Blog post]. Retrieved from www.psolarz.weebly.com/how-to-set-up-and-run-a-mystery-skype-session.html

Tolisano, S. (2014, May 10). Be the Fly on the Wall: Mystery Skype. *Langwitches Blog* [Blog post]. Retrieved from www.langwitches.org/blog/2014/05/10/be-the-fly-on-the-wall-mystery-skype/

Wiebe, G. (2013, December 3). Tip of the Week: Mystery Skype. *History Tech* [Blog post]. Retrieved from www.historytech.wordpress.com/2013/12/06/tip-of-the-week-mystery-skype/

Yollis, L. (2011, June 8). Mystery Skype Call with Langwitches! *Mrs. Yollis' Classroom Blog* [Blog post]. Retrieved from www.yollisclassblog.blogspot.com/2011/06/mystery-skype-call-with-langwitches.html

Yollis, L. (2011, July 20). Langwitches' Video of the Mystery Skype Call. *Mrs. Yollis' Classroom Blog* [Blog post]. Retrieved from www.yollisclassblog.blogspot.com/2011/07/langwitches-video-of-mystery-skype-call.html

Online Resources

Castles Northern Ireland, Virtual Visit Tours: www.virtualvisittours.com/category/castles-northern-ireland/

Dan, Dan the Science Man:

www.dandanscienceman.com

www.dandanscienceman.com/scientists-help-science-teachers-using-social-media/

www.dandanscienceman.com/sci-u-share/

DreamWakers: www.dreamwakers.org/

Twitter Handles of Bibliography Sources

DreamWakers: www.dreamwakers.org/
@pernilleripp (P. Ripp)
@mr_avery (S. Avery)
@PaulSolarz (P. Solarz)
@trockr11 (T. Hart)
@langwitches (S. Tolisano)
@lindayollis (L. Yollis)

Printed in the United States
By Bookmasters